D1055217

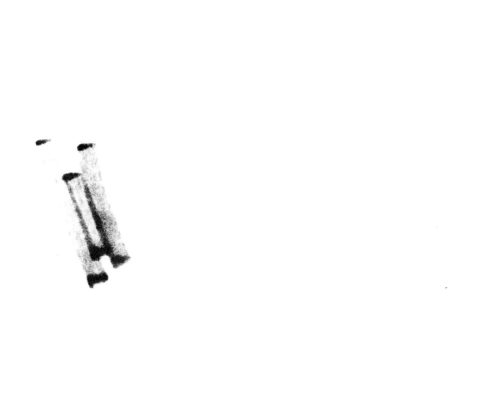

SCIENTIFIC
AMERICAN™
CUTTING-EDGE SCIENCE™

What Makes
a Genius?

ROSEN
PUBLISHING

New York

Published in 2008 by The Rosen Publishing Group, Inc.
29 East 21st Street, New York, NY 10010

The articles in this book first appeared in the pages of *Scientific American*, as follows: "Islands of Genius" by Darold A. Treffert and Gregory L. Wallace, January 2004; "Inside the Mind of a Savant" by Darold A. Treffert and Daniel D. Christensen, December 2005; "Williams Syndrome and the Brain" by Howard M. Lenhoff, Paul P. Wang, Frank Greenberg, and Ursula Bellugi, December 1997; "Manic-Depressive Illness and Creativity" by Kay Redfield Jamison, February 1995; "Uncommon Talents: Gifted Children, Prodigies and Savants" by Ellen Winner, Winter 1998; "Watching Prodigies for the Dark Side" by Marie-Noëlle Ganry-Tardy, April 2005; "The Expert Mind" by Philip E. Ross, August 2006.

First Edition

Library of Congress Cataloging-in-Publication Data

What makes a genius?—1st ed.
    p. cm.—(Scientific American cutting-edge science)
Includes index.
ISBN-13: 978-1-4042-1401-9 (library binding)
1. Genius. 2. Creative ability. 3. Intelligence levels. I. Scientific American.
BF412.W43 2008
153.9'8—dc22

                2007028628

Manufactured in Singapore

Illustration credits: Cover foreground photo © Lara Fisher/i-Stock; p. 28 Sara Chen; pp. 39, 46 Tomo Narashima; pp. 92, 93, 97, 100, 103 Lucy Reading-Ikkanda.

Table of Contents

Introduction

Millions of years of evolution have endowed *Homo sapiens* with remarkable intellect. But not all human brains are created equal. From the great powers of memory seen in savants to the skills of chess grandmasters, unusual talents can offer a unique window on how the mind works. This book examines genius in some of its most intriguing forms.

Meet Kim Peek, whose abilities provided the inspiration for the character Raymond Babbit in the movie *Rain Man*. Peek's severe developmental disabilities prevent him from managing the chores of daily life, but he has learned more than 7,600 books by heart so far, among other astonishing feats of memory. Other savants have musical or artistic talents.

Less well known than savant syndrome is Williams syndrome, a disorder in which affected individuals generally score below average on standard IQ tests, but often possess startling language and music skills, as another article in this issue describes. Mood disorders, too, have been linked to genius: it seems that manic-depressive illness and major depression can enhance creativity in some people.

Other articles focus on gifted children. These youngsters fascinate with their precocious intellect, but they often suffer ridicule and neglect. They also tend to be keenly aware of the potential risk of failure, which can prove emotionally paralyzing for them. Studies of such children have provided key insights into brain development—and revealed how best to nurture their extraordinary minds.

Our final article in the issue considers whether some geniuses are made, not born. Dissections of the mental processes of chess grandmasters have shown that their skills arise from years of "effortful study"—continually tackling challenges that lie just beyond their competence. Could comparable training turn any one of us into such an expert? Food for thought. —*The Editors*

I. "Islands of Genius"

By Darold A. Treffert and Gregory L. Wallace

Artistic brilliance and a dazzling memory can sometimes accompany autism and other developmental disorders.

Leslie Lemke is a musical virtuoso. At the age of 14 he played, flawlessly and without hesitation, Tchaikovsky's Piano Concerto No. 1 after hearing it for the first time while listening to a television movie several hours earlier. Lemke had never had a piano lesson—and he still has not had one. He is blind and developmentally disabled, and he has cerebral palsy. Lemke plays and sings thousands of pieces at concerts in the U.S. and abroad, and he improvises and composes as well.

Richard Wawro's artwork is internationally renowned, collected by Margaret Thatcher and Pope John Paul II, among others. A London art professor was "thunderstruck" by the oil crayon drawings that Wawro did as a child, describing them as an "incredible phenomenon rendered with the precision of a mechanic and the vision of a poet." Wawro, who lives in Scotland, is autistic.

Kim Peek is a walking encyclopedia. He has memorized more than 7,600 books. He can recite the highways that go to each American city, town or county, along with the area and zip codes, television stations and telephone networks that serve them. If you tell him your date of birth, he can tell you what day of the week it fell on and what day of the week it will be when you turn 65 "and can retire." Peek can identify most classical compositions and knows the date the music was published or first performed as well as the composer's birthplace and dates of birth and death. He is also developmentally disabled and depends on his father for many of his basic daily needs. His abilities provided the inspiration for the character Raymond Babbitt, whom Dustin Hoffman played in the 1988 movie *Rain Man*.

Lemke, Wawro and Peek all have savant syndrome, an uncommon but spectacular condition in which people with various developmental disabilities, including autism, possess astonishing islands of ability and brilliance that stand in jarring juxtaposition to their overall mental handicap. Savant syndrome is seen in about one in 10 people with autism and in approximately one in 2,000 people with brain damage or mental retardation. Of the known savants, at least half are autistic and the remainder have some other kind of developmental disorder.

Much remains mysterious about savant syndrome. Nevertheless, advances in brain imaging are permitting a more complete view of the condition, and a long-standing theory of left hemispheric damage has found support in these imaging studies. In addition, new reports of the sudden appearance of savant syndrome in people with certain forms of dementia have raised the intriguing possibility that some aspects of such genius lie dormant in all of us.

Down's Definition

Descriptions of savant syndrome appear in the scientific literature as early as 1789. Benjamin Rush, the "father of American psychiatry," described the lightning-quick calculating ability of Thomas Fuller, who understood little math more complex than counting. When Fuller was asked how many seconds a man had lived by the time he was 70 years, 17 days and 12 hours old, he gave the correct answer of 2,210,500,800 a minute and a half later—and he had taken into account 17 leap years.

It was not until 1887, however, that the remarkable coexistence of deficiency and superiority was more completely laid out. That year J. Langdon Down, who is best known for having identified Down syndrome, described 10 people with savant syndrome. He had met these fascinating individuals during his 30 years as superintendent of the Earlswood Asylum in London. He coined the now discarded term "idiot savant," using the then accepted classification of an idiot as someone with an IQ of less than 25, combined with a derivative of the French word *savoir*, which means "to know."

More than a century has passed since Down's description. Today we know much more about this perplexing set of abilities from the 100 or so cases described in the scientific literature. Savant syndrome generally occurs in people with IQs between 40 and 70—although it can occur in some with IQs up to 114 or even higher. It disproportionately affects males, with four to six male savants for every one female. And it can be congenital or acquired later in life following disease (such as encephalitis) or brain injury.

Narrow Repertoire

The skills that savant syndrome gives rise to are limited for the most part, and they tend to be based in the right hemisphere. That is, they are predominantly nonsymbolic, artistic, visual and motor. They include music, art, mathematics, forms of calculating, and an assortment of other abilities, such as mechanical aptitude or spatial skills. In contrast, left hemisphere skills are more sequential, logical and symbolic; they include language and speech specialization [see "The Split Brain Revisited," by Michael S. Gazzaniga; *Scientific American*, July 1998].

Most musical savants have perfect pitch and perform with amazing ease, most often on the piano. Some are able to create complex compositions. And for some reason, musical genius often seems to accompany blindness and mental retardation, as it does for Lemke. One of the most famous savants was "Blind Tom" Bethune, who lived from 1849 to 1908. In his time, he was referred to as "the eighth wonder of the world." Although he could speak fewer than 100 words, he could play beautifully more than 7,000 pieces on the piano, including many of his own works. (Some of his compositions were recorded by musician John Davis and released in 2000.)

For their part, savant visual artists use a variety of media, although they most frequently express themselves through drawing and sculpture. Artistic savant Alonzo Clemons, for example, can see a fleeting image of an animal on a television screen and in less than 20 minutes sculpt a perfect replica of that animal. His wax model will be correct in every detail, every fiber and muscle and proportion.

Mathematical savants calculate incredibly rapidly and often have a particular facility with prime numbers. Curiously, the obscure skill of calendar calculating that Peek demonstrates is not confined to mathematical savants; it seems to coexist with many different skills.

Several other abilities appear less frequently. A rare savant may have extensive language ability—that is, the capacity to memorize many languages but not to understand them. Other unusual traits include heightened olfactory, tactile and visual sensitivity; outstanding knowledge in fields such as history, neurophysiology, statistics or navigation; and spatial ability. For instance, a musical and blind savant named Ellen can navigate in thick forests or other unfamiliar spaces without running into objects. Ellen also has a perfect appreciation of passing time despite the fact that she doesn't have access to a watch or clock, even in Braille. This ability was discovered one day when her mother let her listen to the "time lady" on the telephone. After listening for a short while to the recorded voice intone the hour and seconds, Ellen apparently set her own internal clock. Since then, she has been able to tell what time it is to the second, no matter the season.

Savant skills are always linked to a remarkable memory. This memory is deep, focused and based on habitual recitation. But it entails little understanding of what is being described. Some early observers aptly called this "memory without reckoning." Down himself used the phrase "verbal adhesion" to characterize it. One of his patients was a boy who had read the six-volume *History of the Decline and Fall of the Roman Empire*, by Edward Gibbon, and could recite it back word for word, although he did so without any comprehension.

Although they share many talents, including memory, savants vary enormously in their levels of ability. So-called splinter-skill savants have a preoccupation and mild expertise with, say, the memorization of sports trivia and license plate numbers. Talented savants have musical or artistic gifts that are conspicuously above what would be expected of someone with their handicaps. And prodigious savants are those very uncommon people whose abilities are so advanced that they would be distinctive even if they were to occur in a normal person. Probably fewer than 50 prodigious savants are alive at the moment.

Whatever their talents, savants usually maintain them over the course of their life. With continued use, the abilities are sustained and sometimes even improve.

And in almost all cases, there is no dreaded trade-off of these wonderful abilities with the acquisition of language, socialization or daily living skills. Instead the talents often help savants to establish some kind of normal routine or way of life [see "Living with Savant Syndrome" box].

Looking to the Left Hemisphere

Although specialists today are better able to characterize the talents of savants, no overarching theory can describe exactly how or why savants do what they do. The most powerful explanation suggests that some injury to the left brain causes the right brain to compensate for the loss. The evidence for this idea has been building for several decades. A 1975 pneumoencephalogram study found left hemispheric damage in 15 of 17 autistic patients; four of them had savant skills. (A pneumoencephalogram was an early and painful imaging technique during which a physician would inject air into a patient's spinal fluid and then x-ray the brain to determine where the air traveled. It is no longer used.)

A dramatic study published by T. L. Brink in 1980 lent further credence to the possibility that changes to the left hemisphere were important to savant syndrome. Brink, a psychologist at Crafton Hills College in California, described a normal nine-year-old boy who had become mute, deaf and paralyzed on the right side when a bullet damaged his left hemisphere. After the accident, unusual savant mechanical skills emerged.

He was able to repair multigeared bicycles and to design contraptions, such as a punching bag that would weave and bob like a real opponent.

The findings of Bernard Rimland of the Autism Research Institute in San Diego support this idea as well. Rimland maintains the largest database in the world on people with autism; he has information on more than 34,000 individuals. He has observed that the savant skills most often present in autistic people are those associated with right hemisphere functions and the most deficient abilities are associated with left hemisphere functions.

In the late 1980s Norman Geschwind and Albert M. Galaburda of Harvard University offered an explanation for some causes of left hemispheric damage—and for the higher number of male savants. In their book *Cerebral Lateralization*, the two neurologists point out that the left hemisphere of the brain normally completes its development later than the right and is therefore subject to prenatal influences—some of them detrimental—for a longer period. In the male fetus, circulating testosterone can act as one of these detrimental influences by slowing growth and impairing neuronal function in the more vulnerable left hemisphere. As a result, the right brain often compensates, becoming larger and more dominant in males. The greater male-to-female ratio is seen not just in savant syndrome but in other forms of central nervous system dysfunction, such as dyslexia, delayed speech, stuttering, hyperactivity and autism.

Newly Savant

In recent years, more data have emerged to support the left hemisphere hypothesis. In 1998 Bruce L. Miller of the University of California at San Francisco examined five elderly patients with frontotemporal dementia (FTD), one form of presenile dementia. These patients had developed artistic skills with the onset and progression of their dementia. They were able to make meticulous copies of artworks and to paint beautifully. Consistent with that in savants, the creativity in these five individuals was visual, not verbal. Single-photon-emission computed tomography (SPECT) showed that injury was predominantly on the left side of the brain. Miller examined seven other patients who had developed musical or artistic ability after the appearance of FTD. He found damage on the left as well.

Miller, Craig Hou, then at Washington University, and others then compared these images with those of a nine-year-old artistic autistic savant named DB. SPECT scans of DB revealed a higher-than-normal blood flow in part of his neocortex but decreased flow in his left temporal lobe. (The neocortex is involved with high-level cognitive function; the temporal lobe is responsible for some aspects of memory and emotion.) Miller is hoping to study other artistic savants to see if the findings hold true for them as well. But the fact that DB and older FTD patients with newfound savant skills have the same pathology is quite striking and suggests that researchers will soon be able to identify precisely the neurological features associated with savant syndrome.

The seemingly limitless memory of savants will most likely be harder to pinpoint physiologically. Mortimer Mishkin of the National Institute of Mental Health has

Living with Savant Syndrome

A few reports in the literature suggest that when savants are encouraged to acquire better language skills they lose their special artistic talents. Perhaps the most famous of these cases is that of Nadia, a girl with autism who by the age of three was producing astounding drawings. When she turned seven, Nadia entered a school for autistic children that focused on verbal abilities; by the time she was a teenager, Nadia was more verbal but could no longer create brilliant and intricate drawings.

This trade-off between talent and language or socialization is not something we have witnessed. Instead the exceptional abilities of savants have proved to be strengths that are built on and used as a conduit toward normalization; these skills have helped individuals develop improved social skills, better language acquisition and greater independence. Savants gain a sense of accomplishment because of their talent; that sense, in turn, allows them to participate more fully in the world. Musical prodigy Leslie Lemke has become more animated, performing concerts and interacting with audiences. Painter Richard Wawro feels delight and excitement when he finishes a work, and he seeks out celebration. And memory wizard Kim Peek has emerged from the social isolation that characterized him before the movie *Rain Man* was made; he now travels the country talking to hundreds of school groups.

Fortunately, simultaneously encouraging savant abilities and normalization is now the generally accepted approach to such individuals' care. Savants are being placed in some classes for the gifted and talented, an opportunity that promotes social growth for both them and their classmates. Some new programs, such as the one at Hope University in Anaheim, Calif., cater entirely to these exceptional individuals. Others include people with similar disorders as well; for example, music and art camps have been established for those with Williams syndrome, many of whom have savantlike musical skills [see "Williams Syndrome and the Brain," page 33]. Nurturing the talent of these people is the most fulfilling approach.

—D.A.T. and G.L.W.

proposed different neural circuits for memory, including a higher-level corticolimbic circuit for what is generally referred to as explicit, semantic or cognitive memory, and a lower-level corticostriatal circuit for the more primitive habit memory referred to as implicit or procedural memory. The memory of savants seems to be the noncognitive habit form.

The same factors that produce left hemispheric damage may be instrumental in producing damage to higher-level memory circuits. As a result, savants may be forced to rely on more primitive, but spared, habit memory circuits. Perhaps brain injuries—whether they result from hormones, disease, or prenatal or subsequent injury—produce in some instances certain right-brain skills linked with habit memory function. In those situations, savant syndrome may appear.

Rain Man in Us All?

The emergence of savantlike skills in people with dementia raises profound questions about the buried potential in all of us. Accordingly, several researchers are seeking to unlock what has been called the "little Rain Man in each of us." One group has used a technique called repetitive transcranial magnetic stimulation (rTMS) in 17 normal individuals, eight male and nine female. Tracy Morrell of the University of South Australia, Robyn L. Young of Flinders University in Adelaide and Michael C. Ridding of Adelaide University applied magnetic stimulation to the area in the left temporal lobe that Miller identified as damaged in his FTD patients.

In its study, the team reports that only two of the participants experienced a series of short-lived skills, such as calendar calculating, artistic ability and enhanced habit memory. Other subjects discovered a new skill here and there, also lasting just a few hours. The researchers suggest that savant skills may be limited to a small percentage of the normal population, much as they are limited to a small percentage of the disabled population.

Nevertheless, many experts believe that real potential exists to tap into islands of savant intelligence. Allan Snyder and John Mitchell of the Australian National University in Canberra argue that savant brain processes occur in each of us but are overwhelmed by more sophisticated conceptual cognition. Autistic savants, they conclude, "have privileged access to lower levels of information not normally available through introspection."

Our view is also that all of us have some of the same circuitry and pathways intrinsic to savant functioning but that these are less accessible—in part because we tend to be a left-brain society. Sometimes, though, we can find elements of the savant in ourselves. At certain moments, we just "get" something or discover a new ability. And some procedures—including hypnosis; interviews of subjects under the influence of the barbiturate sodium amytal, which induces relaxation;

and brain stimulation during neurosurgery—provide evidence that a huge reservoir of memories lies dormant in every individual. Dreams can also revive those memories or trigger new abilities.

No model of brain function will be complete until it can explain this rare condition. Now that we have the tools to examine brain structure and function, such studies can be correlated with detailed neuropsychological testing of savants. We hope the anecdotal case reports that have characterized the literature on this topic for the past century will soon be replaced by data comparing and contrasting groups of normal and disabled people, including prodigies, geniuses and savants.

A Window into the Brain

Savant syndrome provides a unique window into the brain with regard to questions of general intelligence versus multiple forms of intelligence. It may also shed light on brain plasticity and central nervous system compensation, recruitment and repair—areas of research that are vital in understanding and treating such diverse conditions as stroke, paralysis and Alzheimer's disease.

But savant syndrome has relevance outside the scientific realm. Many lessons can be learned from these remarkable people and their equally remarkable families, caretakers, therapists and teachers. One of the greatest lessons is that they have been shaped by far more than neural circuitry. The savants thrive because of the reinforcement provided by the unconditional love, belief and determination of those who care for them. Savant syndrome promises to take us further than we have ever been toward understanding both the brain and human potential.

Further Reading

Emergence of Artistic Talent in Frontotemporal Dementia. B. Miller, J. Cummings and F. Mishkin et al. in *Neurology*, Vol. 51, No. 4, pages 978–982; October 1, 1998.

Extraordinary People: Understanding Savant Syndrome. Darold A. Treffert. iUniverse.com, Inc., 2000.

www.savantsyndrome.com

The Authors

DAROLD A. TREFFERT and *GREGORY L. WALLACE* share a long-standing interest in savant syndrome. Treffert (dtreffert@pol.net) is a clinical professor of psychiatry at the University of Wisconsin–Madison and has done research on autism and savant syndrome since 1962, the year he met his first savant. Wallace (gregwallace@mail.nih.gov) is a research fellow in the Child Psychiatry Branch of the National Institute of Mental Health. He is conducting studies on why individuals with autism are more likely to develop savant skills.

2. "Inside the Mind of a Savant"

By Darold A. Treffert and Daniel D. Christensen

Kim Peek possesses one of the most extraordinary memories ever recorded. Until we can explain his abilities, we cannot pretend to understand human cognition.

When J. Langdon Down first described savant syndrome in 1887, coining its name and noting its association with astounding powers of memory, he cited a patient who could recite Edward Gibbon's *The Decline and Fall of the Roman Empire* verbatim. Since then, in almost all cases, savant memory has been linked to a specific domain, such as music, art or mathematics. But phenomenal memory is itself the skill in a 54-year-old man named Kim Peek. His friends call him "Kim-puter."

He can, indeed, pull a fact from his mental library as fast as a search engine can mine the Internet. He read Tom Clancy's *The Hunt for Red October* in one hour and 25 minutes. Four months later, when asked, he gave the name of the Russian radio operator in the book, referring to the page describing the character and quoting several passages verbatim. Kim began memorizing books at the age of 18 months, as they were read to him. He has learned 9,000 books by heart so far. He reads a page in eight to 10 seconds and places the memorized book upside down on the shelf to signify that it is now on his mental "hard drive."

Kim's memory extends to at least 15 interests—among them, world and American history, sports, movies, geography, space programs, actors and actresses, the Bible, church history, literature, Shakespeare and classical music. He knows all the area codes and zip codes in the U.S., together with the television stations serving those locales. He learns the maps in the front of phone books and can provide Yahoo-like travel directions within any major U.S. city or between any pair of them. He can identify hundreds of classical compositions, tell when and where each was composed and first performed, give the name of the composer and many biographical details, and even discuss the formal and tonal components of the music. Most intriguing of all, he appears to be developing a new skill in middle life. Whereas before he could merely talk about music, for the past two years he has been learning to play it.

It is an amazing feat in light of his severe developmental problems—characteristics shared, in varying extents, by all savants. He walks with a sidelong gait, cannot button his clothes, cannot manage the chores of daily life and has great difficulties with abstraction. Against these disabilities, his talents—which would be extraordinary in any person—shine all the brighter. An explanation of how Kim does what he does would provide better insight into why certain skills, including the ordinarily obscure skill of calendar calculating (always associated with massive memory), occur with such regularity among savants. Recently, when an interviewer offered that he had been born on March 31, 1956, Kim noted, in less than a second, that it was a Saturday on Easter weekend.

Imaging studies of Kim's brain thus far show considerable structural abnormality [see "A Missing Connection?" box]. These findings cannot yet be linked directly to any of his skills; that quest is just beginning. Newer imaging techniques that plot the brain's functions—rather than just its structure—should provide more insight, though. In the meantime, we believe it is worthwhile to document the remarkable things that Kim can do. People like him are not easily found, and it is useful to record their characteristics for future research. Savantism offers a unique window into the mind. If we cannot explain it, we cannot claim full understanding of how the brain functions.

An Unusual Brain

Kim was born on November 11, 1951 (a Sunday, he will tell you). He had an enlarged head, on the back of which was an encephalocele, or baseball-size "blister," which spontaneously resolved. But there were also other brain abnormalities, including a malformed cerebellum. One of us (Christensen) did the initial MRI brain scans on Kim in 1988 and has followed his progress ever since.

The cerebellar findings may account for Kim's problems with coordination and mobility. But more striking still is the absence of a corpus callosum, the sizable stalk of nerve tissue that normally connects

Peek's Peaks

- Great powers of memory run through every known manifestation of savant skill. In the case of Kim Peek, memory is itself the skill.

- Kim's brain exhibits many abnormalities, including an absent corpus callosum. The role of that particular abnormality in Kim's case remains to be explained, but it evokes a question raised by the skills of all savants: Does brain damage stimulate compensatory development in some other area of the brain, or does it simply allow otherwise latent abilities to emerge?

- Kim's rote learning later developed into a form of associative thinking, with clear evidence of creativity. His success then helped him engage the wider world. The authors conclude that savant skills should never be dismissed but should be cultivated for the patient's intellectual and social development.

the left and right halves of the brain. We do not know what to make of this defect, because although it is rare, it is not always accompanied by functional disorders. Some people have been found to lack the structure without suffering any detectable problems at all. Yet in people whose corpus callosum has been severed in adulthood, generally in an effort to prevent epileptic seizures from spreading from one hemisphere to the other, a characteristic "split-brain" syndrome arises in which the estranged hemispheres begin to work almost independently of each other.

It would seem that those born without a corpus callosum somehow develop back channels of communication between the hemispheres. Perhaps the resulting structures allow the two hemispheres to function, in certain respects, as one giant hemisphere, putting functions normally rather separate under the same roof, as it were. If so, then Kim may owe some of his talents to this particular abnormality. In any case, the fact that some people lacking a corpus callosum suffer no disabilities, whereas others have savant abilities, makes its purpose less clear than formerly thought. Neurologists joke that its only two certain functions are to propagate seizures and hold the brain together.

Theory guides us in one respect. Kim's brain shows abnormalities in the left hemisphere, a pattern found in many savants. What is more, left hemisphere damage has been invoked as an explanation of why males are much more likely than females to display not only savantism but also dyslexia, stuttering, delayed speech, and autism. The proposed mechanism has two parts: male fetuses have a higher level of circulating testosterone, which can be toxic to developing brain tissue; and the left hemisphere develops more slowly than the right and therefore remains vulnerable for a longer period. Also supporting the role of left hemisphere damage are the many reported cases of "acquired savant syndrome," in which older children and adults suddenly develop savant skills after damage to the left hemisphere.

What does all this evidence imply? One possibility is that when the left hemisphere cannot function properly, the right hemisphere compensates by developing new skills, perhaps by recruiting brain tissue normally ear-marked for other purposes. Another possibility is that injury to the left hemisphere merely unveils skills that had been latent in the right hemisphere all along, a phenomenon some have called a release from the "tyranny" of the dominant left hemisphere.

Kim underwent psychological testing in 1988. His overall IQ score was 87, but the verbal and performance subtests varied greatly, with some scores falling in the superior range of intelligence and others in the mentally retarded range. The psychological report concluded, therefore, that "Kim's IQ classification is not a valid description of his intellectual ability." The "general intelligence" versus "multiple intelligences" debate rages on in psychology. We believe that Kim's case argues for the latter point of view.

Kim's overall diagnosis was "developmental disorder not otherwise specified," with no diagnosis of autistic disorder. Indeed, although autism is more commonly linked with savantism than is any other single disorder, only about half of all savants are autistic. In contrast with autistic people, Kim is outgoing and quite personable. One thing that does seem necessary for the full development of savant skills is a strong interest in the subject matter in question.

Memory and Music

In Kim's case, all the interests began in rote memorization but later progressed to something more. Although Kim generally has a limited capacity for abstract or conceptual thinking—he cannot, for example, explain many commonplace proverbs—he does comprehend much of the material he has committed to memory. This degree of comprehension is unusual among savants. Down himself coined the interesting phrase "verbal adhesion" to describe the savant's ability to remember huge quantities of words without comprehension. Sarah Parker, a graduate student in psychology at the University of Pennsylvania, in a description of a savant named Gordon stated it more colorfully when she noted that "owning a kiln of bricks does not make one a mason." Kim not only owns a large kiln of bricks, he has also become a strikingly creative and versatile word mason within his chosen areas of expertise.

Sometimes his answers to questions or directions are quite concrete and literal. Once when asked by his father in a restaurant to "lower his voice," Kim merely slid lower into his chair, thus lowering his voice box. In other cases, his answers can seem quite ingenious. In one of his talks he answered a question about Abraham Lincoln's Gettysburg Address by responding, "Will's house, 227 North West Front Street. But he stayed there only one night—he gave the speech the next day." Kim intended no joke, but when his questioner laughed, he saw the point; since then, he has purposely recycled the story with humorous intent and effect.

Yet Kim does have an undeniable power to make clever connections. He once attended a Shakespeare festival sponsored by a philanthropist known by the initials O.C., whose laryngitis threatened to keep him from acknowledging a testimonial. Kim—a fan of

Shakespeare, and like him, an incorrigible punster—quipped, "O.C., can you say?"

Such creative use of material that had originally been memorized by rote can be seen as the verbal equivalent of a musician's improvisation. Like the musician, Kim thinks quickly, so quickly that it can be difficult to keep up with his intricate associations. Often he seems two or three steps ahead of his audiences in his responses.

A rather startling new dimension to Kim's savant skills has recently surfaced. In 2002 he met April Greenan, director of the McKay Music Library and professor of music at the University of Utah. With her help, he soon began to play the piano and to enhance his discussion of compositions by playing passages from them, demonstrating on the keyboard many of the pieces he recalled from his massive mental library. Kim also has remarkable long-term memory of pitch, remembering the original pitch level of each composition.

He possesses complete knowledge of the instruments in the traditional symphony orchestra and readily identifies the timbre of any instrumental passage. For example, he presented the opening of Bedrich Smetana's orchestral tone poem *The Moldau*, by reducing the flute and clarinet parts to an arpeggiated figure in his left hand and explaining that the oboes and bassoons enter with the primary theme, which he then reduced to pitches played singly and then in thirds by his right hand (the left-hand figure continuing as it does in the score). His comprehension of musical styles is demonstrated in his ability to identify composers of pieces he had not previously heard by assessing the piece's musical style and deducing who that composer might be.

Though Kim is still physically awkward, his manual dexterity is increasing. When seated at the piano, he may play the piece he wishes to discuss, sing the passage of

A Missing Connection?

Kim Peek's brain differs from typical brains in several ways. Kim's brain and head are very large, each in the 99th percentile. Most striking is the complete absence of the corpus callosum, which normally connects the left and right hemispheres. Missing, too, are the anterior and posterior commissures, which also usually link the hemispheres. The cerebellum, responsible for certain motor functions, is smaller than usual and malformed, with fluid occupying much of the surrounding space; this may explain some of Kim's difficulties with coordination. What role these abnormalities play in his mental abilities is the subject of investigation.

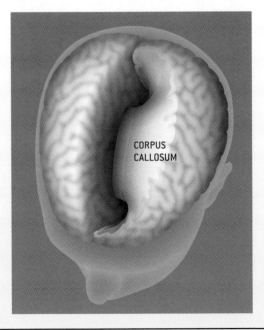

CORPUS CALLOSUM

interest or describe the music verbally, shifting seamlessly from one mode to another. Kim pays attention to rhythm as well, lightly tapping the beat on his chest with his right hand or, when playing, tapping his right foot.

Greenan, a Mozart scholar, makes these observations: "Kim's knowledge of music is considerable. His ability to recall every detail of a composition he has heard—in many cases only once and more than 40 years ago—is astonishing. The connections he draws between and weaves through compositions, composer's lives, historical events, movie soundtracks and thousands of facts stored in his database reveal enormous intellectual capacity." She even compares him to Mozart, who also had an enlarged head, a fascination with numbers and uneven social skills. She wonders whether Kim might even learn to compose.

Life after Rain Man

It is not surprising that Kim's prodigious memory caught the attention of writer Barry Morrow at a chance meeting in 1984 and inspired him to write the screenplay for *Rain Man*, whose main character, Raymond Babbitt, is a savant played by Dustin Hoffman. The movie is purely fictional and does not tell Kim's life story, even in outline. But in one remarkably prescient scene, Raymond instantly computes square roots in his head, and his brother, Charlie, remarks, "He ought to work for NASA or something." For Kim, such a collaboration might well happen.

NASA has proposed to make a high-resolution 3-D anatomical model of Kim's brain architecture. Richard Boyle, director of the NASA BioVIS Technology Center, describes the project as part of a larger effort to overlay and fuse image data from as wide a range of brains as possible—and that is why Kim's unusual brain is of particular value. The data, both static and functional, should enable investigators to locate and identify changes in the brain that accompany thought and behavior. NASA hopes that this detailed model will enable physicians to improve their ability to interpret output from far less capable ultrasound imaging systems, which are the only kind that can now be carried into space and used to monitor astronauts.

The filming of *Rain Man* and the movie's subsequent success proved to be a turning point in Kim's life. Before then, he had been reclusive, retreating to his room when company came; afterward, the confidence he gained from his contacts with the filmmakers, together with the celebrity provided by the movie's success, inspired him and his father, Fran Peek, to share Kim's talents with many audiences. They became enthusiastic emissaries for people with disabilities, and over the years they have shared their story with more than 2.6 million people.

We believe that Kim's transformation has general applicability. Much of what scientists know about health comes out of the study of pathologies, and certainly much of what will be learned about normal memory will come from the study of unique or unusual memory. In the meantime, we draw some practical conclusions for the care of other persons with special needs who have some savant skill. We recommend that family and other caregivers "train the talent," rather than dismissing such skills as frivolous, as a means for the savant to connect with other people and mitigate the effects of the disability. It is not an easy path, because disability and limitations still require a great deal of dedication, patience and hard work—as Kim's father, by his example, so convincingly demonstrates.

Further exploration of savant syndrome will provide both scientific insights and stories of immense human interest. Kim Peek provides ample evidence of both.

More to Explore

The Real Rain Man. Fran Peek. Harkness Publishing Consultants, 1996.

Extraordinary People: Understanding Savant Syndrome. Reprint edition. Darold A. Treffert. iUniverse, Inc., 2000.

Islands of Genius. Darold A. Treffert and Gregory L. Wallace in *Scientific American*, Vol. 286, No. 6, pages 76–85; June 2002.

www.savantsyndrome.com, a Web site maintained by the Wisconsin Medical Society.

The Authors

DAROLD A. TREFFERT and *DANIEL D. CHRISTENSEN* have long been fascinated by savantism. Treffert, a psychiatrist in Wisconsin, has done research on autism and savant syndrome since 1962, the year he first met a savant. He was consultant to the movie *Rain Man* and is author of *Extraordinary People: Understanding Savant Syndrome*. Christensen is clinical professor of psychiatry, clinical professor of neurology and adjunct professor of pharmacology at the University of Utah Medical School. His work focuses on Alzheimer's disease, but following Kim Peek for more than two decades has given him an ongoing interest in savant syndrome.

"Williams Syndrome
3. and the Brain"

By Howard M. Lenhoff, Paul P. Wang, Frank Greenberg,
and Ursula Bellugi

*To gain fresh insights into how the brain is organized, investigators are
turning to a little known disorder.*

When a teenager with an IQ of just 49 was asked
to draw an elephant and tell what she knew about the
animal, her sketch was almost indecipherable. But her
description was impressively rich, even lyrical. As part
of that description, she noted, "It has long, gray ears,
fan ears, ears that can blow in the wind . . . ."

In her verbal ability, that young woman is fairly
typical of people who have Williams syndrome, a rare
condition that has recently started to draw the attention
of a range of scientists. Affected individuals, sometimes
called Williams people, are not all alike but often are
similar to one another. They are frequently diagnosed
as mildly to moderately "retarded" and generally score
below average on standard IQ tests. They usually read
and write poorly and struggle with simple arithmetic.
Yet they display striking strengths in some realms. They
generally demonstrate a facility not only for spoken
language but also for recognizing faces. And, as a group,
they tend to be empathetic, loquacious and sociable.

What is more, anecdotal evidence implies that some
Williams people possess extraordinary musical talent.
Even though their attention span for most tasks is short,

many will listen to music, sing and play instruments with astonishing persistence. Most cannot read musical notes, yet some have perfect or nearly perfect pitch and an uncanny sense of rhythm. One boy quickly learned to play an extremely complex drumbeat in 7/4 time with one hand while drumming in 4/4 time with the other hand. A number of individuals retain complex music for years, remembering melodies and verses of long ballads; one even sings songs in 25 languages. Experienced Williams musicians also sing harmonies, improvise and compose lyrics readily.

Such anecdotes have recently led to the first systematic study of musical ability in Williams children. The results indicate that the youngsters discriminate melodies well; they also show significantly more interest in and emotional responsivity to music than do subjects from the general population. As one Williams child said, "Music is my favorite way of thinking."

Investigators are attracted to Williams syndrome in part because they suspect the dramatic peaks and valleys in the abilities of affected individuals will provide a new window to the organization and adaptability of the normal brain. Some groups are attempting to pinpoint characteristic properties of the Williams brain and to determine how those properties influence performance in intellectual and other realms. At the same time, researchers are trying to uncover the genetic abnormalities responsible for Williams syndrome.

In 1993 they learned that the disorder is caused by loss of a tiny piece from one of the two copies of chromosome 7 present in every cell of the body. The deleted piece can contain 15 or more genes. As the lost genes are identified, scientists can begin to determine how their absence leads to the neuroanatomical and behavioral features already observed. This integrated approach to the study of Williams syndrome—connecting genes to neurobiology and, ultimately, to behavior—may become a model for exploring how genes affect brain development and function.

Medical scientists are interested in Williams syndrome in its own right as well. Analysis of the genes in the deleted region has already explained why Williams people commonly suffer from certain physical ailments. It has also provided a means of prenatal testing and is helping to diagnose the disorder earlier, so that children who are affected can be helped from infancy to live up to their fullest potential; lack of familiarity with Williams syndrome in medical circles and the absence of reliable tests have hindered prompt diagnosis in the past.

Understanding Grew Slowly

Although Williams syndrome, which occurs in an estimated one in 20,000 births worldwide, has gained increased attention lately, it is not by any means new. An investigation by one of us (Lenhoff) suggests that Williams people were the inspiration for some age-old folktales about elves, pixies and other "wee people" [see "Williams Syndrome: An Inspiration for Some Pixie legends?" box].

The medical community became aware of the syndrome fairly recently, however—only about 40 years ago. In 1961 J.C.P. Williams, a heart specialist in New Zealand, noted that a subset of his pediatric patients shared many characteristics. Beyond having related cardiovascular problems, they also had elfin facial features (such as a turned-up nose and a small chin) and seemed to be mentally retarded. The cardiac problems Williams observed often included heart murmurs and narrowing of major blood vessels. In particular, Williams people frequently suffer from supravalvular aortic stenosis (SVAS), a mild to severe constriction of the aorta.

Since that time, physicians have noted other traits, some of which can be seen quite early in life. In infancy, babies may have difficulty feeding and may suffer from stomach pains, constipation and hernias. They may also sleep poorly and can be irritable and colicky, behavior sometimes caused by another frequent sign: elevated amounts of calcium in the blood. As the children get older, they reveal hoarse voices and show delayed physical and mental development. They begin walking at an average of 21 months, often on the balls of their feet and usually with an awkwardness that persists throughout life. Fine motor control is disturbed as well. In addition, Williams people are extremely sensitive to noise, are often short compared with their peers and seem to age prematurely (for instance, their hair grays and their skin wrinkles relatively early).

Description began to give way to genetic under-standing about four years ago, thanks in part to a

Williams Syndrome:
An Inspiration for Some Pixie Legends?

Folktales from many cultures feature magical "little people"—pixies, elves, trolls and other fairies. A number of physical and behavioral similarities suggest that at least some of the fairies in the early yarns were modeled on people who have Williams syndrome. Such a view is in keeping with the contention of historians that a good deal of folklore and mythology is based on real life.

The facial traits of Williams people are often described as pixielike. In common with pixies in folklore and art, many with Williams syndrome have small, upturned noses, a depressed nasal bridge, "puffy" eyes, oval ears and broad mouths with full lips accented by a small chin. Indeed, those features are so common that Williams children tend to look more like one another than their relatives, especially as children. The syndrome also is accompanied by slow growth and development, which leads most Williams individuals to be relatively short.

The "wee, magical people" of assorted folktales often are musicians and story-tellers. Fairies are said to "repeat the songs they have heard" and can "enchant" humans with their melodies. Much the same can be said of people with Williams syndrome, who in spite of typically having subnormal IQs, usually display vivid narrative skills and often show talent for music. (The large pointed ears so often associated with fairies may symbolically represent the sensitivity of those mythical individuals—and of Williams people—to music and to sound in general.)

As a group, Williams people are loving, trusting, caring and extremely sensitive to the feelings of others. Similarly, fairies are frequently referred to as the "good people" or as kind and gentle-hearted souls. Finally, Williams individuals, much like the fairies of legend, require order and predictability. In Williams people this need shows up as rigid adherence to daily routines and a constant need to keep abreast of future plans.

In the past, storytellers created folktales about imaginary beings to help explain phenomena that they did not understand—perhaps including the distinguishing physical and behavioral traits of Williams syndrome. Today researchers turn to Williams people in a quest to understand the unknown, hoping to decipher some of the secrets of how the brain functions.

—H.M.L.

study of SVAS in people who did not have Williams syndrome. In 1993 Amanda K. Ewart and Mark T. Keating of the University of Utah, Colleen A. Morris of the University of Nevada and other collaborators discovered that for a segment of this population, SVAS stemmed from an inherited mutation in one copy of the gene that gives rise to elastin—a protein that provides elasticity to many organs and tissues, such as the arteries, lungs, intestines and skin.

Missing Genes Are Identified

Aware that SVAS is common in Williams people and that individuals with familial SVAS alone and individuals with Williams syndrome both suffer disturbances in organs that require elasticity, the workers wondered whether Williams syndrome, too, involved some kind of change in the gene for elastin. Sure enough, they found the gene was deleted from one of the two copies of chromosome 7 in cells. Today it is evident that the deletion of the gene occurs in approximately 95 percent of patients with Williams syndrome. The loss is harmful presumably because both gene copies are needed to make adequate amounts of the elastin protein.

The investigators knew that a reduction in the elastin supply could contribute to various physical features of Williams syndrome (such as SVAS, hernias and premature wrinkling), but it could not by itself account for the cognitive and behavioral signatures. After all, their first subjects, who had SVAS alone without cognitive impairment, would also have had low IQs if a diminution of elastin could unilaterally produce all the symptoms of Williams syndrome. This awareness led them to suspect that more genes were affected. In support of that idea, direct examinations of chromosomes from Williams patients indicated that the region deleted from chromosome 7 extended beyond the boundaries of the gene for elastin and probably encompassed many genes.

Several of those other genes are now being uncovered. Among them are three (*LIM-kinase 1*, *FZD3* and *WSCR1*) that are active in the brain—a sign that they could influence brain development and function. The exact activities carried out by the encoded proteins are not known, although Ewart and her colleagues have proposed that *LIM-kinase 1* (which is invariably deleted with the gene for elastin) may be involved in the ability to grasp spatial relationships. This role could help explain why Williams people have difficulty drawing

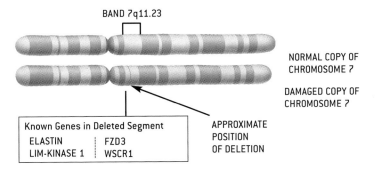

BAND 7q11.23

NORMAL COPY OF CHROMOSOME 7

DAMAGED COPY OF CHROMOSOME 7

Known Genes in Deleted Segment	
ELASTIN	FZD3
LIM-KINASE 1	WSCR1

APPROXIMATE POSITION OF DELETION

Tiny deletion from one of the two copies of chromosome 7 in cells is the cause of Williams syndrome (*drawing*). The excised region can contain 15 or more genes, only some of which have been identified. A diagnostic test is based on the discovery that the gene for elastin is usually among those lost. The test flags copies of chromosome 7 with a fluorescent green tag and flags the gene for elastin with a fluorescent red tag.

simple common objects accurately from memory. Another gene from the deleted area, *RFC2*, specifies a protein involved in replication of DNA, but its contribution to Williams syndrome has not been established.

The genetic understanding of Williams syndrome is far from complete. Still, discovery of the deletion in chromosome 7 has yielded some practical rewards. That the deletion occurs in all cells of the body in Williams people tells mothers nothing they did or failed to do during pregnancy caused their child's condition. The disorder stems from a sperm or egg that, by chance, suffers a loss of genes from chromosome 7 before donating its chromosomes to the creation of an embryo. That knowledge also tells healthy siblings of Williams people that their copies of chromosome 7 are free of the deletion; therefore, any children they bear are no more likely than other children to acquire Williams syndrome. Finally, the microscopic technique that originally revealed the deletion of the gene for elastin—fluorescent in situ hybridization, or FISH—has now been adapted for use as a diagnostic tool.

A Cognitive Problem Emerges

Work on the genetics of Williams syndrome is complementing efforts to specify the neurobiological hallmarks of the disorder. That research, which today involves several laboratories, began about 15 years ago, when one of us (Bellugi) answered a late-night telephone call in her laboratory at the Salk Institute for Biological Studies in La Jolla, Calif. The caller knew that Bellugi investigated the neurobiological underpinnings of language and believed her daughter, who had Williams syndrome, would interest the Salk group. The girl, then 13, had an IQ near 50 and was considered mentally retarded. Consistent with that profile, she read and wrote at the level of a first grader. Yet she spoke beautifully.

Then, as now, scientists had difficulty distinguishing the brain processes controlling language from those controlling reasoning, because in the general population, adeptness at language and cognition usually go hand in hand. The dichotomy in the caller's daughter suggested that study of Williams people might help tease apart those processes.

Fascinated, Bellugi agreed to meet the girl and then continued to see her regularly. She also sought literature detailing the cognitive strengths and weaknesses of Williams people but found little beyond general assertions. Before Bellugi could hope to uncover the areas of the brain and the neurological processes that accounted for the unique cognitive characteristics of Williams people, she would need a finer-grained profile of the traits distinguishing that population from others. She and her colleagues therefore began to devise tests of specific abilities and to compare the scores of Williams people with those of the general population and of another cognitively impaired group: people with Down syndrome.

The investigations, which continue, examine populations of adolescents matched for sex, age and IQ level. (Williams people range in IQ from 40 to 100, but their mean score is about 60.) Early on, the team saw that Williams subjects, in contrast to their generally weak performance on overall tests of cognitive ability, commonly used well-formed grammar in their spontaneous speech. On the whole, they also performed significantly better than the group with Down syndrome did on all tasks of grammatical comprehension and production.

Many also did well at the rather complex task of constructing tag questions, such as adding "doesn't she?" to the statement "Leslie likes fish." The person being tested must first take the original statement ("Leslie likes fish") and substitute a matching pronoun for the subject ("*She* likes fish"). Then the individual must add a conjugated auxiliary verb, negate it and contract it ("She *doesn't* like fish"), omit the original verb and object (leaving only "She doesn't") and invert the word order to form a question (". . . , doesn't she?").

The Salk researchers further found, as others did later, that the Williams subjects frequently had vocabularies larger than would be expected for their mental age. When asked to list some animals, they often did not stick to easy words but chose such exotic examples as yak, Chihuahua, ibex, condor and unicorn.

Beyond possessing richer vocabularies, subjects with Williams syndrome tended to be more expressive than

even normal children were. This animation was demonstrated amusingly when Williams children were asked to
provide a story for a series of wordless pictures. As they
told their tale, they often altered their pitch, volume,
length of words or rhythm to enhance the emotional
tone of the story. Similarly, they added more drama to
engage their audience ("And suddenly, splash!;" "And
BOOM!;" "Gadzooks!") than subjects with Down
syndrome did. (Sadly, the gift of gab and sociability
of Williams children can mislead teachers into thinking
the children have better reasoning skills than they
actually possess; in those cases, the children may not
get the academic support they need.)

One possible explanation for the strong verbal
performance of Williams individuals is that their
chromosomal defect, in contrast to that of Down
subjects, may not significantly disrupt certain faculties
that support language processing. Other researchers, for
instance, have reported that short-term memory for
speech sounds, or "phonological working memory"—
a form that seems to assist in language learning and
comprehension—is relatively preserved in the Williams
population.

Interestingly, recent studies of French and Italian
Williams subjects suggest that one aspect of language
known as morphology—the facet of grammar that
deals with verb conjugation, gender assignment and
pluralization—may not be completely preserved in
Williams people. (These languages are much richer in

morphology than English is.) This discovery implies that the brain regions preserved in Williams syndrome and the presence of an intact short-term memory for speech sounds support many verbal aptitudes but may not suffice for full mastery of language.

In contrast to their generally good showing on verbal tests, Williams subjects typically do poorly on tasks involving visual processing, such as copying drawings. But they often fail on such tasks in different ways than Down subjects do, suggesting that the deficits in the two groups may stem from differences in brain anatomy. For example, Williams people, in common with patients who have suffered a stroke in the right hemisphere of the brain, may attend to components of images but fail to appreciate the overall pattern (the gestalt). Down people, however, are more likely to perceive the global organization but to overlook many details, just as individuals do who have suffered left-hemisphere strokes.

In some ways, the general profile revealed by the various cognitive tests implies that the chromosomal defect in Williams syndrome essentially spares the left hemisphere (the region most important to language in the large majority of people) and disrupts the right (the more visual-spatial hemisphere). But the emotional expressiveness of Williams people (also thought to be a right-sided function) and at least one other finding cast doubt on that simplistic view. Williams people recognize and discriminate among pictures of unfamiliar faces (a

skill that requires the right hemisphere) remarkably
well. In fact, they perform as well as adults from the
general population.

Neurological Studies Add Clarity

The Salk group's examination of brains by magnetic
resonance imaging and by autopsy supports the prob-
ability that the chromosomal deletion responsible for
Williams syndrome alters the brain in a more complicated way. The deletion seems to produce anatomical
changes (such as abnormal clustering of neurons in
visual areas) that yield deficits in visual-spatial abilities.
But the chromosomal defect appears to spare a network
that includes structures in the frontal lobes, the temporal
lobe and the cerebellum. This preserved network, then,
may serve as a neuroanatomical scaffolding for the
unexpectedly strong language abilities of Williams people.

To be more specific, the neuroanatomical studies
indicate that the overall cortical volume in both Williams
and Down people is smaller than that of age-matched
normal subjects. But the volumes of individual regions
differ between the two groups. For instance, the frontal
lobes and the limbic region of the temporal lobes are
better preserved in Williams people. The limbic system,
which also includes other structures, is important for
brain activities involving memory and emotions; sparing
of the limbic region may help explain why Williams
people are quite expressive and empathetic.

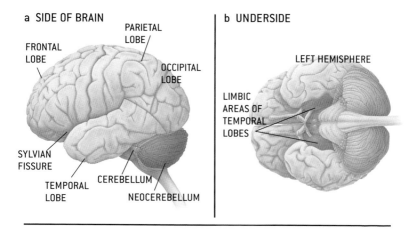

a SIDE OF BRAIN

PARIETAL LOBE

FRONTAL LOBE

OCCIPITAL LOBE

SYLVIAN FISSURE

TEMPORAL LOBE

CEREBELLUM

NEOCEREBELLUM

b UNDERSIDE

LEFT HEMISPHERE

LIMBIC AREAS OF TEMPORAL LOBES

c CUT IN PLANE OF SYLVIAN FISSURE

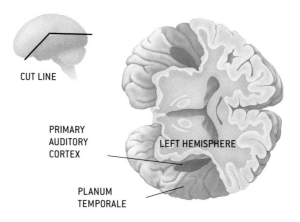

CUT LINE

PRIMARY AUDITORY CORTEX

LEFT HEMISPHERE

PLANUM TEMPORALE

Basic anatomy of brain in people with Williams syndrome is normal, but the total volume is somewhat reduced. The areas that seem to be best preserved include the frontal lobes and a part of the cerebellum called the neocerebellum (a), as well as parts of the temporal lobes known as the limbic area (b), the primary auditory area and the planum temporale (c).

Analyses of the cerebellum uncovered further differences between the Williams and Down groups. Whereas its volume in Down subjects was small, that in Williams subjects was normal. And in Williams subjects the neocerebellum (considered to be the evolutionarily youngest region of the cerebellum) was equal to or larger than that in age-matched individuals in the general population but was reduced in Down subjects.

The finding that the neocerebellum is preserved in Williams people is particularly intriguing when placed in the context of other research. Until recently, the cerebellum was thought to be concerned primarily with movement. Yet Steven E. Petersen and his colleagues at Washington University have shown that the neocerebellum becomes active when subjects try to think of a verb that fits with a given noun (such as "sit" for "chair"). Further, tests of patients with cerebellar injuries reveal deficits in cognitive function, not just in motor abilities. And anatomists report that the neocerebellum communicates extensively with a part of the frontal cortex that, in common with the neocerebellum, is larger in humans than in apes.

Given that humans have language and apes do not, some observers have proposed that the neocerebellum and the connected region of the frontal cortex evolved together to support the fluent processing of speech and may fall under the control of the same genes. The relative preservation of the frontal cortex and the enlargement of the neocerebellum in Williams people, together with the rather spared fluency in language, lend some credence to this last notion and to the idea that the cerebellum plays a part in language processing.

Recent anatomical analyses have additionally identified features that could help explain the apparent musical talent of Williams people. The primary auditory cortex (located in the temporal lobe) and an adjacent auditory region, the planum temporale (thought to be important to language as well as musicality), are proportionately enlarged in the few Williams brains examined so far. In addition, the planum temporale is normally more extensive in the left hemisphere than in the right, but in some Williams people the left region is unusually big, to an extent characteristic of professional musicians. These findings mesh well with observations by Audrey Don of the University of Windsor in Ontario, the investigator who carried out the first studies of musical ability in Williams people. She concludes that intact perception of auditory patterns may account for much of the strength in music and language seen in Williams subjects—a result that implies the related brain structures should also be intact.

Physiological probes comparing electrical activity in the brains of Williams people and others during specific tasks offer more insights into how the brain develops. In response to grammatical stimuli, for example, normal subjects show greater activity from the left hemisphere than from the right, as would be expected for language tasks. But Williams people show symmetrical responses in the two hemispheres, a sign that the typical language specialization of the left hemisphere has not occurred. Further, whereas normal adults generally show greater activity from the right hemisphere than the left when processing images of faces, Williams people show the opposite pattern. Such work favors the possibility that when normal developmental processes go awry, the brain often redistributes responsibilities, forming new circuits to carry out the functions of the disrupted ones.

Research into Williams syndrome is just now taking off, but it is already helping to clarify how the brain is organized. It is also making investigators see "mentally retarded" individuals in a new light. Close study of Williams syndrome has shown that low IQ scores can mask the existence of exciting capacities. And it warns that other so-called mentally retarded individuals could have untapped potentials waiting to be uncovered—if only researchers, and society, will take the trouble to look for and cultivate them.

Further Reading

Hemizygosity at the Elastin Locus in a Developmental Disorder: Williams Syndrome. A. K. Ewart et al. in *Nature Genetics*, Vol. 5, No. 1, pages 11–16; September 1993.

Cognitive and Neural Development: Clues from Genetically Based Syndromes. U. Bellugi, E. S. Klima and P. P. Wang in *The Lifespan Development of*

Individuals: *Behavioral, Neurobiological, and Psychosocial Perspectives: A Synthesis.* Nobel Symposium. Edited by D. Magnusson. Cambridge University Press, 1996.

Real-World Source for the "Little People": The Relationship of Fairies to Individuals with Williams Syndrome. Howard M. Lenhoff in *Nursery Realms: Children in the Worlds of Science Fiction, Fantasy and Horror.* Edited by Gary Westfahl and George Slusser. University of Georgia (in press).

The Authors

HOWARD M. LENHOFF, PAUK P. WANG, FRANK GREENBERG and *URSULA BELLUGI* offer several perspectives on Williams syndrome. Lenhoff is professor emeritus of biological sciences at the University of California, Irvine, the father of a 42-year-old Williams syndrome musician and co-organizer of the Williams Syndrome Music and Arts Camp, held in Massachusetts. He is also principal investigator of a team comparing music cognition in Williams people with other populations. Wang, assistant professor of pediatrics at the University of Pennsylvania School of Medicine, studies the neurobehavioral manifestations of Williams syndrome and other genetic disorders. Greenberg, clinical consultant with the National Center for Human Genome Research at the National Institutes of Health, has worked with Williams syndrome individuals for 20 years. Bellugi is director of the Laboratory for Cognitive Neurosciences at the Salk Institute for Biological Studies. She heads a multidisciplinary team that has been examining the cognitive, neuroanatomical and neurophysiological characteristics of Williams syndrome for more than a decade.

4. "Manic-Depressive Illness and Creativity"

by Kay Redfield Jamison

Does some fine madness plague great artists?
Several studies now show that creativity and mood disorders are linked.

"Men have called me mad," wrote Edgar Allan Poe, "but the question is not yet settled, whether madness is or is not the loftiest intelligence—whether much that is glorious—whether all that is profound—does not spring from disease of thought—from moods of mind exalted at the expense of the general intellect."

Many people have long shared Poe's suspicion that genius and insanity are entwined. Indeed, history holds countless examples of "that fine madness." Scores of influential 18th- and 19th-century poets, notably William Blake, Lord Byron and Alfred, Lord Tennyson, wrote about the extreme mood swings they endured. Modern American poets John Berryman, Randall Jarrell, Robert Lowell, Sylvia Plath, Theodore Roethke, Delmore Schwartz and Anne Sexton were all hospitalized for either mania or depression during their lives. And many painters and composers, among them Vincent van Gogh, Georgia O'Keeffe, Charles Mingus and Robert Schumann, have been similarly afflicted.

Judging by current diagnostic criteria, it seems that most of these artists—and many others besides—

suffered from one of the major mood disorders, namely, manic-depressive illness or major depression. Both are fairly common, very treatable and yet frequently lethal diseases. Major depression induces intense melancholic spells, whereas manic-depression, a strongly genetic disease, pitches patients repeatedly from depressed to hyperactive and euphoric, or intensely irritable, states. In its milder form, termed cyclothymia, manic-depression causes pronounced but not totally debilitating changes in mood, behavior, sleep, thought patterns and energy levels. Advanced cases are marked by dramatic, cyclic shifts.

Could such disruptive diseases convey certain creative advantages? Many people find that proposition counter-intuitive. Most manic-depressives do not possess extraordinary imagination, and most accomplished artists do not suffer from recurring mood swings. To assume, then, that such diseases usually promote artistic talent wrongly reinforces simplistic notions of the "mad genius." Worse yet, such a generalization trivializes a very serious medical condition and, to some degree, discredits individuality in the arts as well. It would be wrong to label anyone who is unusually accomplished, energetic, intense, moody or eccentric as manic-depressive. All the same, recent studies indicate that a high number of established artists—far more than could be expected by chance—meet the diagnostic criteria for manic-depression or major depression given in the fourth edition of the *Diagnostic and Statistical Manual of Mental Disorders (DSM-IV)*. In fact, it seems that these diseases can sometimes enhance or otherwise contribute to creativity in some people.

By virtue of their prevalence alone, it is clear that mood disorders do not necessarily breed genius. Indeed, 1 percent of the general population suffer from manic-depression, also called bipolar disorder, and 5 percent from a major depression, or unipolar disorder, during their lifetime. Depression affects twice as many women as men and most often, but not always, strikes later in life. Bipolar disorder afflicts equal numbers of women and men, and more than a third of all cases surface before age 20. Some 60 to 80 percent of all adolescents and adults who commit suicide have a history of bipolar or unipolar illness. Before the late 1970s, when the drug lithium first became widely available, one person in five with manic-depression committed suicide.

Major depression in both unipolar and bipolar disorders manifests itself through apathy, lethargy, hopelessness, sleep disturbances, slowed physical

The Case of Vincent Van Gogh

Many clinicians have reviewed the medical and psychiatric problems of the painter Vincent van Gogh posthumously, diagnosing him with a range of disorders, including epilepsy, schizophrenia, digitalis and absinthe poisoning, manic-depressive psychosis, acute intermittent porphyria and Ménière's disease.

Richard Jed Wyatt of the National Institute of Mental Health and I have argued in detail that van Gogh's symptoms, the natural course of his illness and his family psychiatric history strongly indicate manic-depressive illness. The extent of the artist's purported use of absinthe and convulsive behavior remains unclear; in any event, his psychiatric symptoms long predate any possible history of seizures. It is possible that he suffered from both an epileptic disorder and manic-depressive illness.   —K. R. J.

movements and thinking, impaired memory and concentration, and a loss of pleasure in typically enjoyable events. The diagnostic criteria also include suicidal thinking, self-blame and inappropriate guilt. To distinguish clinical depression from normal periods of unhappiness, the common guidelines further require that these symptoms persist for a minimum of two to four weeks and also that they significantly interfere with a person's everyday functioning.

Mood Elevation

During episodes of mania or hypomania (mild mania), bipolar patients experience symptoms that are in many ways the opposite of those associated with depression. Their mood and self-esteem are elevated. They sleep less and have abundant energy; their productivity increases. Manics frequently become paranoid and irritable. Moreover, their speech is often rapid, excitable and intrusive, and their thoughts move quickly and fluidly from one topic to another. They usually hold tremendous conviction about the correctness and importance of their own ideas as well. This grandiosity can contribute to poor judgment and impulsive behavior.

Hypomanics and manics generally have chaotic personal and professional relationships. They may spend large sums of money, drive recklessly or pursue questionable business ventures or sexual liaisons. In some cases, manics suffer from violent agitation and delusional thoughts as well as visual and auditory hallucinations.

Rates of Mood Disorders

For years, scientists have documented some kind of connection between mania, depression and creative output. In the late 19th and early 20th centuries, researchers turned to accounts of mood disorders written by prominent artists, their physicians and friends. Although largely anecdotal, this work strongly suggested that renowned writers, artists and composers—and their first-degree relatives—were far more likely to experience mood disorders and to commit suicide than was the general population. During the past 20 years, more systematic studies of artistic populations have confirmed these findings. Diagnostic and psychological analyses of living writers and artists can give quite meaningful estimates of the rates and types of psychopathology they experience.

In the 1970s Nancy C. Andreasen of the University of Iowa completed the first of these rigorous studies, which made use of structured interviews, matched control groups and strict diagnostic criteria. She examined 30 creative writers and found an extraordinarily high occurrence of mood disorders and alcoholism among them. Eighty percent had experienced at least one episode of major depression, hypomania or mania; 43 percent reported a history of hypomania or mania. Also, the relatives of these writers, compared with the relatives of the control subjects, generally performed more creative work and more often had a mood disorder.

A few years later, while on sabbatical in England from the University of California at Los Angeles, I began a study of 47 distinguished British writers and visual artists. To select the group as best I could for creativity, I purposefully chose painters and sculptors who were Royal Academicians or Associates of the Royal Academy. All the playwrights had won the New York Drama Critics Award or the Evening Standard Drama (London Critics) Award, or both. Half of the poets were already represented in the *Oxford Book of Twentieth Century English Verse.* I found that 38 percent of these artists and writers had in fact been previously treated for a mood disorder; three fourths of those treated had required medication or hospitalization, or both. And half of the poets—the largest fraction from any one group—had needed such extensive care.

Hagop S. Akiskal of the University of California at San Diego, also affiliated with the University of Tennessee at Memphis, and his wife, Kareen Akiskal, subsequently interviewed 20 award-winning European writers, poets, painters and sculptors. Some two thirds of their subjects exhibited recurrent cyclothymic or hypomanic tendencies, and half had at one time suffered from a major depression. In collaboration with David H. Evans of the University of Memphis, the Akiskals noted the same trends among living blues musicians. More recently Stuart A. Montgomery and his wife, Deirdre B. Montgomery, of St. Mary's Hospital in London examined 50 modern British poets. One fourth met current diagnostic criteria for depression or manic-depression; suicide was six times more frequent in this community than in the general population.

Ruth L. Richards and her colleagues at Harvard University set up a system for assessing the degree of original thinking required to perform certain creative tasks. Then, rather than screening for mood disorders among those already deemed highly inventive, they attempted to rate creativity in a sample of manic-depressive patients. Based on their scale, they found that compared with individuals having no personal or family history of psychiatric disorders, manic-depressive and cyclothymic patients (as well as their unaffected relatives) showed greater creativity.

Biographical studies of earlier generations of artists and writers also show consistently high rates of suicide, depression and manic-depression—up to 18 times the rate of suicide seen in the general population, eight to 10 times that of depression and 10 to 20 times that of manic-depressive illness and its milder variants. Joseph J. Schildkraut and his co-workers at Harvard concluded that approximately half of the 15 20th-century abstract-expressionist artists they studied suffered from depressive or manic-depressive illness; the suicide rate in this group was at least 13 times the current U.S. national rate.

In 1992 Arnold M. Ludwig of the University of Kentucky published an extensive biographical survey of 1,005 famous 20th-century artists, writers and other professionals, some of whom had been in treatment for a

The Tainted Blood of the Tennysons

Alfred, Lord Tennyson, who experienced recurrent, debilitating depressions and probable hypomanic spells, often expressed fear that he might inherit the madness, or "taint of blood," in his family. His father, grandfather, two of his great-grandfathers as well as five of his seven brothers suffered from insanity, melancholia, uncontrollable rage or what is today known as manic-depressive illness. His brother Edward was confined to an asylum for nearly 60 years before he died from manic exhaustion. Lionel Tennyson, one of Alfred's two sons, displayed a mercurial temperament, as did one of his three grandsons.

Modern medicine has confirmed that manic-depression and creativity tend to run in certain families. Studies of twins provide strong evidence for the heritability of manic-depressive illness. If an identical twin has manic-depressive illness, the other twin typically has a 70 to 100 percent chance of also having the disease; if the other twin is fraternal, the chances are considerably lower (approximately 20 percent). A review of pairs of identical twins reared apart from birth—in which at least one had been diagnosed as manic-depressive—found that in two thirds or more of the sets, the illness was present in both twins.

—K. R. J.

mood disorder. He discovered that the artists and writers experienced two to three times the rate of psychosis, suicide attempts, mood disorders and substance abuse that comparably successful people in business, science and public life did. The poets in this sample had most often been manic or psychotic and hospitalized; they also proved to be some 18 times more likely to commit suicide than is the general public. In a comprehensive biographical study of 36 major British poets born between 1705 and 1805, I found similarly elevated rates of psychosis and severe psychopathology. These poets were 30 times more likely to have had manic-depressive illness than were their contemporaries, at least 20 times more likely to have been committed to an asylum and some five times more likely to have taken their own life.

These corroborative studies have confirmed that highly creative individuals experience major mood disorders more often than do other groups in the general population. But what does this mean for their work? How does a psychiatric illness contribute to creative achievement? First, the common features of hypomania seem highly conducive to original thinking; the diagnostic criteria for this phase of the disorder include "sharpened and unusually creative thinking and increased productivity." And accumulating evidence suggests that the cognitive styles associated with hypomania (expansive thought and grandiose moods) can lead to increased fluency and frequency of thoughts.

Mania and Creativity

Studying the speech of hypomanic patients has revealed that they tend to rhyme and use other sound associations, such as alliteration, far more often than do unaffected individuals. They also use idiosyncratic words nearly three times as often as do control subjects. Moreover, in specific drills, they can list synonyms or form other word associations much more rapidly than is considered normal. It seems, then, that both the quantity and quality of thoughts build during hypomania. This speed increase may range from a very mild quickening to complete psychotic incoherence. It is not yet clear what causes this qualitative change in mental processing. Nevertheless, this altered cognitive state may well facilitate the formation of unique ideas and associations.

People with manic-depressive illness and those who are creatively accomplished share certain noncognitive features: the ability to function well on a few hours of sleep, the focus needed to work intensively, bold and restless attitudes, and an ability to experience a profound depth and variety of emotions. The less dramatic daily aspects of manic-depression might also provide creative advantage to some individuals. The manic-depressive temperament is, in a biological sense, an alert, sensitive system that reacts strongly and swiftly. It responds to the world with a wide range of emotional, perceptual, intellectual, behavioral and energy changes. In a sense, depression is a view of the world through a dark glass, and mania is that seen through a kaleidoscope—often brilliant but fractured.

Where depression questions, ruminates and hesitates, mania answers with vigor and certainty. The constant transitions in and out of constricted and then expansive thoughts, subdued and then violent responses, grim and then ebullient moods, withdrawn and then outgoing stances, cold and then fiery states—and the rapidity and fluidity of moves through such contrasting experiences—can be painful and confusing. Ideally, though, such chaos in those able to transcend it or shape it to their will can provide a familiarity with transitions that is probably useful in artistic endeavors. This vantage readily accepts ambiguities and the counteracting forces in nature.

Extreme changes in mood exaggerate the normal tendency to have conflicting selves; the undulating, rhythmic and transitional moods and cognitive changes so characteristic of manic-depressive illness can blend or harness seemingly contradictory moods, observations and perceptions. Ultimately, these fluxes and yokings may reflect truth in humanity and nature more accurately than could a more fixed viewpoint. The "consistent attitude toward life" may not, as Byron scholar Jerome J. McGann of the University of Virginia points out, be as insightful as an ability to live with, and portray, constant change.

The ethical and societal implications of the association between mood disorders and creativity are important but poorly understood. Some treatment strategies pay insufficient heed to the benefits manic-depressive illness can bestow on some individuals. Certainly most manic-depressives seek relief from the disease, and lithium and anticonvulsant drugs are very effective therapies for manias and depressions. Nevertheless, these drugs can dampen a person's general intellect and limit his or her emotional and perceptual range. For this reason, many manic-depressive patients stop taking these medications.

Left untreated, however, manic-depressive illness often worsens over time—and no one is creative when severely depressed, psychotic or dead. The attacks of both mania and depression tend to grow more frequent and more severe. Without regular treatment the disease eventually becomes less responsive to medication. In addition, bipolar and unipolar patients frequently abuse mood-altering substances, such as alcohol and illicit drugs, which can cause secondary medical and emotional burdens for manic-depressive and depressed patients.

The Goal of Treatment

The real task of imaginative, compassionate and effective treatment, therefore, is to give patients more meaningful choices than they are now afforded. Useful intervention must control the extremes of depression and psychosis without sacrificing crucial human emotions and experiences. Given time and increasingly sophisticated research, psychiatrists will likely gain a better understanding of the complex biological basis for mood disorders. Eventually, the development of new drugs should make it possible to treat manic-depressive individuals so that those aspects of temperament and cognition that are essential to the creative process remain intact.

The development of more specific and less problematic therapies should be swift once scientists find the gene, or genes, responsible for the disease. Prenatal tests and other diagnostic measures may then become available; these possibilities raise a host of complicated ethical issues. It would be irresponsible to romanticize such a painful, destructive and all too often deadly disease. Hence, 3 to 5 percent of the Human Genome Project's total budget (which is conservatively estimated at $3 billion) has been set aside for studies of the social, ethical and legal implications of genetic research. It is hoped that these investigations will examine the troubling issues surrounding manic-depression and major depression at length. To help those who have manic-depressive illness, or who are at risk for it, must be a major public health priority.

Further Reading

Tennyson: The Unquiet Heart. R. B. Martin. Oxford University Press, 1980.

Creativity and Mental Illness: Prevalence Rates in Writers and Their First-Degree Relatives. Nancy C. Andreasen in *American Journal of Psychiatry*, Vol. 144, No. 10, pages 1288–1292; October 1987.

Manic Depressive Illness. Frederick K. Goodwin and Kay R. Jamison. Oxford University Press, 1990.

Creative Achievement and Psychopathology: Comparison among Professions. Arnold M. Ludwig in *American Journal of Psychiatry*, Vol. 46, No. 3, pages 330–356; July 1992.

Touched with Fire: Manic-Depressive Illness and the Artistic Temperament. Kay R. Jamison. Free Press/Macmillan, 1993.

The Author

KAY REDFIELD JAMISON is professor of psychiatry at the Johns Hopkins University School of Medicine. She wrote *Touched with Fire: Manic-Depressive Illness and the Artistic Temperament* and co-authored the medical text *Manic-Depressive Illness.* Jamison is a member of the National Advisory Council for Human Genome Research and clinical director of the Dana Consortium on the Genetic Basis of Manic-Depressive Illness. She has also written and produced a series of public television specials about manic-depressive illness and the arts.

"Uncommon Talents: Gifted Children, Prodigies
5. and Savants"

By Ellen Winner

Possessing abilities well beyond their years, gifted children inspire admiration, but they also suffer ridicule, neglect and misunderstanding.

One evening a few years ago, while I was attending a concert, a young boy in the audience caught my attention. As the orchestra played a Mozart concerto, this nine-year-old child sat with a thick, well-thumbed orchestral score opened on his lap. As he read, he hummed the music out loud, in perfect tune. During intermission, I cornered the boy's father. Yes, he told me, Stephen was really reading the music, not just looking at it. And reading musical scores was one of his preferred activities, vying only with reading college-level computer programming manuals. At an age when most children concentrate on fourth-grade arithmetic and the nuances of playground etiquette, Stephen had already earned a prize in music theory that is coveted by adults.

Gifted children like Stephen are fascinating but also intimidating. They have been feared as "possessed," they have been derided as oddballs, they have been ridiculed as nerds. The parents of such young people are often criticized for pushing their children rather than allowing them a normal, well-balanced childhood. These children are so different from others that schools usually do not know how to educate them. Meanwhile society expects gifted children to become creative intellectuals and artists as adults and views them as failures if they do not.

Psychologists have always been interested in those who deviate from the norm, but just as they know more about psychopathology than about leadership and courage, researchers also know far more about retardation than about giftedness. Yet an understanding of the most talented minds will provide both the key to educating gifted children and a precious glimpse of how the human brain works.

The Nature of Giftedness

Everyone knows children who are smart, hard-working achievers—youngsters in the top 10 to 15 percent of all students. But only the top 2 to 5 percent of children are gifted. Gifted children (or child prodigies, who are just extreme versions of gifted children) differ from bright children in at least three ways:

- **Gifted children are precocious.**
  They master subjects earlier and learn more quickly than average children do.

- **Gifted children march to their own drummer.**
  They make discoveries on their own and can often intuit the solution to a problem without going through a series of logical, linear steps.

- **Gifted children are driven by "a rage to master."** They have a powerful interest in the area, or domain, in which they have high ability— mathematics, say, or art—and they can readily focus so intently on work in this domain that they lose sense of the outside world.

These are children who seem to teach themselves to read as toddlers, who breeze through college mathematics in middle school or who draw more skillfully as second-graders than most adults do. Their fortunate combination of obsessive interest and an ability to learn easily can lead to high achievement in their chosen domain. But gifted children are more susceptible to interfering social and emotional factors than once was thought.

The first comprehensive study of the gifted, carried out over a period of more than 70 years, was initiated at Stanford University in the early part of this century by Lewis M. Terman, a psychologist with a rather rosy opinion of gifted children. His study tracked more than 1,500 high-IQ children over the course of their lives. To qualify for the study, the "Termites" were first nominated by their teachers and then had to score 135 or higher on the Stanford-Binet IQ test (the average score is 100). These children were precocious: they typically spoke early, walked early and read before they entered school. Their parents described them as being insatiably curious and as having superb memories.

Terman described his subjects glowingly, not only as superior in intelligence to other children but also as superior in health, social adjustment and moral attitude. This conclusion easily gave rise to the myth that gifted children are happy and well adjusted by nature, requiring little in the way of special attention—a myth that still guides the way these children are educated today.

In retrospect, Terman's study was probably flawed. No child entered the study unless nominated by a teacher as one of the best and the brightest; teachers probably overlooked those gifted children who were misfits, loners or problematic to teach. And the shining evaluations of social adjustment and personality in the gifted were performed by the same admiring teachers who had singled out the study subjects. Finally, almost a third of the sample came from professional, middle-class families. Thus, Terman confounded IQ with social class.

The myth of the well-adjusted, easy-to-teach gifted child persists despite more recent evidence to the contrary. Mihaly Csikszentmihalyi of the University of Chicago has shown that children with exceptionally high abilities in any area—not just in academics but in the visual arts, music, even athletics—are out of step with their peers socially. These children tend to be highly driven, independent in their thinking and introverted. They spend more than the usual amount of time alone, and although they derive energy and pleasure from their solitary mental lives, they also report feeling lonely. The more extreme the level of gift, the more isolated these children feel.

Contemporary researchers have estimated that about 20 to 25 percent of profoundly gifted children have social and emotional problems, which is about twice the normal rate; in contrast, moderately gifted children do not exhibit a higher than average rate. By middle childhood, gifted children often try to hide their abilities in the hopes of becoming more popular. One group particularly at risk for such underachievement is academically gifted girls, who report more depression, lower self-esteem and more psychosomatic symptoms than academically gifted boys do.

The combination of precocious knowledge, social isolation and sheer boredom in many gifted children is a tough challenge for teachers who must educate them alongside their peers. Worse, certain gifted children can leap years ahead of their peers in one area yet fall behind in another. These children, the unevenly gifted, sometimes seem hopelessly out of sync.

The Unevenly Gifted

Terman was a proponent of the view that gifted children are globally gifted—evenly talented in all academic areas. Indeed, some special children have exceptional verbal skills as well as strong spatial, numerical and logical skills that enable them to excel in mathematics. The occasional child who completes college as an early teen—or even as a preteen—is likely to be globally gifted. Such children are easy to spot: they are all-around high achievers. But many children exhibit gifts in one area of study and are unremarkable or even learning disabled in others. These may be creative children who are difficult in school and who are not immediately recognized as gifted.

Unevenness in gifted children is quite common. A recent survey of more than 1,000 highly academically gifted adolescents revealed that more than 95 percent show a strong disparity between mathematical and verbal interests. Extraordinarily strong mathematical and spatial abilities often accompany average or even deficient verbal abilities. Julian Stanley of Johns Hopkins University has found that many gifted children selected for special summer programs in advanced math have enormous discrepancies between their math and verbal skills. One such eight-year-old scored 760 out of a perfect score of 800 on the math part of the Scholastic Assessment Test (SAT) but only 290 out of 800 on the verbal part.

In a retrospective analysis of 20 world-class mathematicians, psychologist Benjamin S. Bloom, then at the University of Chicago, reported that none of his subjects had learned to read before attending school (yet most academically gifted children do read before school) and that six had had trouble learning to read. And a retrospective study of inventors (who presumably exhibit high mechanical and spatial aptitude) showed that as children these individuals struggled with reading and writing.

Indeed, many children who struggle with language may have strong spatial skills. Thomas Sowell of

Stanford University, an economist by training, conducted a study of late-talking children after he raised a son who did not begin to speak until almost age four. These children tended to have high spatial abilities—they excelled at puzzles, for instance—and most had relatives working in professions that require strong spatial skills. Perhaps the most striking finding was that 60 percent of these children had engineers as first- or second-degree relatives.

The association between verbal deficits and spatial gifts seems particularly strong among visual artists. Beth Casey of Boston College and I have found that college art students make significantly more spelling errors than college students majoring either in math or in verbal areas such as English or history. On average, the art students not only misspelled more than half of a 20-word list but also made the kind of errors associated with poor reading skills—nonphonetic spellings such as "physicain" for "physician" (instead of the phonetic "fisician").

The many children who possess a gift in one area and are weak or learning disabled in others present a conundrum. If schools educate them as globally gifted, these students will continually encounter frustration in their weak areas; if they are held back because of their deficiencies, they will be bored and unhappy in their strong fields. Worst, the gifts that these children do possess may go unnoticed entirely when frustrated, unevenly gifted children wind up as misfits or troublemakers.

Savants: Uneven in the Extreme

The most extreme cases of spatial or mathematical gifts coexisting with verbal deficits are found in savants. Savants are retarded (with IQs between 40 and 70) and are either autistic or show autistic symptoms. "Ordinary" savants usually possess one skill at a normal level, in contrast to their otherwise severely limited abilities. But the rarer savants—fewer than 100 are known—display one or more skills equal to prodigy level.

Savants typically excel in visual art, music or lightning-fast calculation. In their domain of expertise, they resemble child prodigies, exhibiting precocious skills, independent learning and a rage to master. For instance, the drawing savant named Nadia sketched more realistically at ages three and four than any known child prodigy of the same age. In addition, savants will often surpass gifted children in the accuracy of their memories.

Savants are like extreme versions of unevenly gifted children. Just as gifted children often have mathematical

Mozart

Wolfgang Amadeus Mozart is among the best-known child prodigies. He began picking out tunes on the piano at three years of age; by four he could tell if a violin was a quarter tone out of tune, and by eight he could play without hesitation a complex piece he had never seen before. Mozart began composing at the age of five, when he wrote two minuets for the harpsichord. Even as a young child, he could play pieces perfectly from memory, having heard them only once, and improvise on a theme without ever repeating himself.

or artistic genius and language-based learning disabilities, savants tend to exhibit a highly developed visual-spatial ability alongside severe deficits in language. One of the most promising biological explanations for this syndrome posits atypical brain organization, with deficits in the left hemisphere of the brain (which usually controls language) offset by strengths in the right hemisphere (which controls spatial and visual skills).

According to Darold A. Treffert, a psychiatrist now in private practice in Fond du Lac, Wis., the fact that many savants were premature babies fits well with this notion of left-side brain damage and resultant right-side compensation. Late in pregnancy, the fetal brain undergoes a process called pruning, in which a large number of excess neurons die off [see "The Developing Brain," by Carla J. Shatz; *Scientific American*, September 1992]. But the brains of babies born prematurely may not have been pruned yet; if such brains experience trauma to the left hemisphere near the time of birth, numerous uncommitted neurons elsewhere in the brain might

Thomas Edison

Thomas Alva Edison exemplifies the unevenly gifted individual. Edison was a prolific inventor, obtaining 1,093 patents for innovations ranging from the phonograph to the incandescent light. As a child, he was obsessed with science and spent much time tinkering in a chemistry laboratory in his parents' cellar. Edison had some difficulties learning, though, especially in the verbal areas; he may have had symptoms of dyslexia. The coexistence of strong spatial-logical skills with a weakness in language is common in the unevenly gifted.

remain to compensate for the loss, perhaps leading to a strong right-hemisphere ability.

Such trauma to a premature infant's brain could arise many ways—from conditions during pregnancy, from lack of oxygen during birth, from the administration of too much oxygen afterward. An excess of oxygen given to premature babies can cause blindness in addition to brain damage; many musical savants exhibit the triad of premature birth, blindness and strong right-hemisphere skill.

Gifted children most likely possess atypical brain organization to some extent as well. When average students are tested to see which part of their brain controls their verbal skills, the answer is generally the left hemisphere only. But when mathematically talented children are tested the same way, both the left and right hemispheres are implicated in controlling language— the right side of their brains participates in tasks ordinarily reserved for the left. These children also tend not to be strongly right-handed, an indication that their left hemisphere is not clearly dominant.

The late neurologist Norman Geschwind of Harvard Medical School was intrigued by the fact that individuals with pronounced right-hemisphere gifts (that is, in math, music, art) are disproportionately nonright-handed (left-handed or ambidextrous) and have higher than average rates of left-hemisphere deficits such as delayed onset of speech, stuttering or dyslexia. Geschwind and his colleague Albert Galaburda theorized that this association of gift with disorder, which they called the "pathology of superiority," results from the effect of the hormone testosterone on the developing fetal brain.

Geschwind and Galaburda noted that elevated testosterone can delay development of the left hemisphere of the fetal brain; this in turn might result in compensatory right-hemisphere growth. Such "testosterone poisoning" might also account for the larger number of males than females who exhibit mathematical and spatial gifts, nonright-handedness and pathologies of language. The researchers also noted that gifted children tend to suffer more than the usual frequency of immune disorders such as allergies and asthma; excess testosterone can interfere with the development of the thymus gland, which plays a role in the development of the immune system.

Testosterone exposure remains a controversial explanation for uneven gifts, and to date only scant evidence from the study of brain tissue exists to support the theory of damage and compensation in savants. Nevertheless, it seems certain that gifts are hardwired in the infant brain, as savants and gifted children exhibit extremely high abilities from a very young age—before they have spent much time working at their gift.

Emphasizing Gifts

Given that many profoundly gifted children are unevenly talented, socially isolated and bored with school, what is the best way to educate them? Most gifted programs today tend to target children who have tested above

130 or so on standard IQ tests, pulling them out of their regular classes for a few hours each week of general instruction or interaction. Unfortunately, these programs fail the most talented students.

Generally, schools are focusing what few resources they have for gifted education on the moderately academically gifted. These children make up the bulk of current "pull-out" programs: bright students with strong but not extraordinary abilities, who do not face the challenges of precocity and isolation to the same degree as the profoundly gifted. These children—and indeed most children—would be better served if schools instead raised their standards across the board.

Other nations, including Japan and Hungary, set much higher academic expectations for their children than the U.S. does; their children, gifted or not, rise to the challenge by succeeding at higher levels. The needs of moderately gifted children could be met by simply teaching them a more demanding standard curriculum.

The use of IQ as a filter for gifted programs also tends to tip these programs toward the relatively abundant, moderately academically gifted while sometimes overlooking profoundly but unevenly gifted children. Many of those children do poorly on IQ tests, because their talent lies in either math or language, but not both. Students whose talent is musical, artistic or athletic are regularly left out as well. It makes more sense to identify the gifted by examining past achievement in specific areas rather than relying on plain-vanilla IQ tests.

Schools should then place profoundly gifted children in advanced courses in their strong areas only. Subjects in which a student is not exceptional can continue to be taught to the student in the regular classroom. Options for advanced classes include arranging courses especially for the gifted, placing gifted students alongside older students within their schools, registering them in college courses or enrolling them in accelerated summer programs that teach a year's worth of material in a few weeks.

Profoundly gifted children crave challenging work in their domain of expertise and the companionship of individuals with similar skills. Given the proper stimulation and opportunity, the extraordinary minds of these children will flourish.

About the Author

ELLEN WINNER was a student of literature and painting before she decided to explore developmental psychology. Her inspiration was Harvard University's Project Zero, which researched the psychological aspects of the arts. Her graduate studies allowed her to combine her interests in art and writing with an exploration of the mind. She received her Ph.D. in psychology from Harvard in 1978 and is currently professor of psychology at Boston College as well as senior research associate with Project Zero.

One of Winner's greatest pleasures is writing books;
she has authored three, one on the psychology of the
arts, another on children's use of metaphor and irony
and, most recently, *Gifted Children: Myths and Realities*.
"I usually have several quite different projects going at
once, so I am always juggling," she remarks. She is
especially intrigued by unusual children—children who
are gifted, learning disabled, gifted and learning disabled,
nonright-handed or particularly creative. "The goal is
to understand cognitive development in its typical and
atypical forms."

When she has time to play, Winner devours novels
and movies and chauffeurs her 13-year-old son on
snowboarding dates. She is married to the psychologist
Howard Gardner and has three grown stepchildren.

6. "Watching Prodigies for the Dark Side"

by Marie-Noëlle Ganry-Tardy

Gifted children who are not challenged can quickly grow bored with school, but a hidden fear of failure can lead to far greater problems.

Jeffrey is just not interested in elementary school anymore. He doesn't retain what he is taught, and his grades are bad. At recess he avoids classmates and keeps to himself. He knows his parents are disappointed in him, too. His teacher finally recommends that he be taken to a child psychiatrist for evaluation. The therapist administers a special intelligence test, and Jeffrey turns out to have an IQ of 150—far above the average for his age. He is a highly gifted child.

Two to 3 percent of children are considered highly gifted, showing IQ scores of at least 130. For many such youngsters, their extraordinary intellect gives them a real advantage in school. They may shine in music, math or science. Contrary to popular belief, child prodigies do not on average have more school or social problems than their less gifted peers, according to longitudinal studies. They may have fewer friends, but that is usually because they make greater demands of acquaintances.

And yet there is a dark side. For some of the most talented—those with IQs in the 140 to 150 range—their gifts can turn out to be a trap. Because these children are so insightful at such a young age, able to make sense of adult ideas, they are constantly aware of the potential risk of failure. This awareness can immobilize them to the point of emotional paralysis, a quiet demon that parents and teachers must watch for.

School tests pose one example. Unlike classmates who typically approach exams with a certain detachment and answer one question at a time, some highly gifted children relentlessly consider the implications of each answer and what the risks are of making an error. Jeffrey's behavior reflected this constant sense of imminent failure. His fear caused his academic performance to be barely average. He also kept himself away from the other children because he doubted they would accept him.

Developmental disorders can exacerbate the trap. Dyslexia affects about 10 percent of children, regardless of their intelligence. The consequences are particularly severe for a highly gifted child. From the moment such a child enters school, he finds that he gets poor grades even though he comprehends everything easily. He therefore encounters difficulty understanding *why* his efforts meet with so little success. A steady diet of frustration eats at his self-esteem. The consequence is anxiety that may even shade into depression. As a defense, the child gradually loses interest in schoolwork and begins to isolate himself from social interaction. Punishment may only make matters worse. With their well-developed sense of right and wrong, prodigies consider punishment undeserved, and they may withdraw further.

Moreover, with their heightened self-awareness, gifted children keenly feel a personal loss caused by any developmental disorders. For example, highly gifted children may be acutely aware of a lack of physical coordination or spatial orientation, which also undermines their self-image.

In some cases, IQ tests mislead parents and teachers as well. A gifted child might excel in questions that probe verbal intelligence, say, but perform miserably on spatial reasoning skills in the labyrinth part of the test. Because both scores are typically combined, the overall result may be just average. The discrepancy between the child's own high expectations and the discouraging evaluation from the adult world may lead a boy or girl up a blind alley that is hard to resolve. The ironic and unfortunate result is that an extremely intelligent child may fail dramatically in school.

Catch It Early

So what is to be done? The first step is to recognize exceptional intelligence as well as developmental disorders so that parents and teachers can intervene. Earlier detection means quicker correction. For instance, in five-year-olds, phonics training can clear up dyslexia within six to 18 months. But if treatment begins only a year later, the correction can take twice as long—extending the chance that the child gives up on school.

Whether a child's spatial orientation is age-appropriate can be demonstrated by comparing performance on the verbal and nonverbal sections of an IQ test. If the nonverbal result is more than 10 points below the verbal result, psychomotor training is recommended. Drawings, games and sculpting can help a child learn to coordinate his movements and improve spatial orientation. This kind of training is also most effective when begun by age five or six.

If the discrepancy between verbal and nonverbal IQ tests is greater than 20 percent, family therapy should also be considered, to improve interaction among family members. During the sessions, the therapist will try to assess how the child has developed and how the testing discrepancy might have arisen. Sometimes a child with motor or orientation problems will be afraid of simple daily tasks, such as tying her shoes. She knows she will probably make mistakes and have to start over—perhaps enduring ridicule from siblings, parents or friends. If the parents try to help, they are unwittingly increasing her dependence on Mommy or Daddy. Yet if they are not around, she will quickly feel abandoned. To help the child regain her sense of independence, the therapist will try to get her to understand that failure is a normal part of life and not a catastrophe.

Child prodigies may also distort their own personalities to the point where they become unrecognizable. Psychiatrists call this the development of a false self. This problem may occur because these extraordinarily sensitive young people often feel deeply the subtle reactions of family members. As a result, they may overinterpret even the slightest sign of dissatisfaction.

To please their parents, they deny their own needs and behave in a way they think matches their parents' expectations. They all but disappear behind a mask of compliance. To prevent this development of a false self, parents should offer a highly gifted child several varied activities and accept without judgment whatever the child chooses to pursue. It is important to encourage a child's special interests so that she does not lose motivation or a willingness to work.

Knowing the potential pitfalls within a child prodigy's world, and how to counter them, can significantly improve each girl and boy's chances for success with their double-edged gifts. And society will be more likely to benefit from their future contributions, whether in art, science, public service or wherever their brilliance leads them.

About the Author

MARIE-NOËLLE GANRY-TARDY is a child psychiatrist in private practice in Paris who specializes in solving the problems of young gifted children.

7. "The Expert Mind"

By Philip E. Ross

Studies of the mental processes of chess grandmasters have revealed clues to how people become experts in other fields as well.

A man walks along the inside of a circle of chess tables, glancing at each for two or three seconds before making his move. On the outer rim, dozens of amateurs sit pondering their replies until he completes the circuit. The year is 1909, the man is José Raúl Capablanca of Cuba, and the result is a whitewash: 28 wins in as many games. The exhibition was part of a tour in which Capablanca won 168 games in a row.

How did he play so well, so quickly? And how far ahead could he calculate under such constraints? "I see only one move ahead," Capablanca is said to have answered, "but it is always the correct one."

He thus put in a nutshell what a century of psychological research has subsequently established: much of the chess master's advantage over the novice derives from the first few seconds of thought. This rapid, knowledge-guided perception, sometimes called apperception, can be seen in experts in other fields as well. Just as a master can recall all the moves in a game he has played, so can an accomplished musician often reconstruct the score to a sonata heard just once.

And just as the chess master often finds the best move in a flash, an expert physician can sometimes make an accurate diagnosis within moments of laying eyes on a patient.

But how do the experts in these various subjects acquire their extraordinary skills? How much can be credited to innate talent and how much to intensive training? Psychologists have sought answers in studies of chess masters. The collected results of a century of such research have led to new theories explaining how the mind organizes and retrieves information. What is more, this research may have important implications for educators. Perhaps the same techniques used by chess players to hone their skills could be applied in the classroom to teach reading, writing and arithmetic.

The *Drosophila* of Cognitive Science

The history of human expertise begins with hunting, a skill that was crucial to the survival of our early ancestors. The mature hunter knows not only where the lion has been; he can also infer where it will go. Tracking skill increases, as repeated studies show, from childhood onward, rising in "a linear relationship, all the way out to the mid-30s, when it tops out," says John Bock, an anthropologist at California State University, Fullerton. It takes less time to train a brain surgeon.

Without a demonstrably immense superiority in skill over the novice, there can be no true experts, only laypeople with imposing credentials. Such, alas, are all too common. Rigorous studies in the past two decades have shown that professional stock pickers invest no more successfully than amateurs, that noted connoisseurs distinguish wines hardly better than yokels, and that highly credentialed psychiatric therapists help patients no more than colleagues with less advanced degrees. And even when expertise undoubtedly exists—as in, say, teaching or business management—it is often hard to measure, let alone explain.

Skill at chess, however, can be measured, broken into components, subjected to laboratory experiments and readily observed in its natural environment, the tournament hall. It is for those reasons that chess has served as the greatest single test bed for theories of thinking—the "*Drosophila* of cognitive science," as it has been called.

The measurement of chess skill has been taken further than similar attempts with any other game, sport or competitive activity. Statistical formulas weigh a player's recent results over older ones and discount successes according to the strength of one's opponents. The results are ratings that predict the outcomes of games with remarkable reliability. If player A outrates player B by 200 points, then A will on average beat B 75 percent of the time. This prediction holds true whether the players are top-ranked or merely ordinary.

Lessons From Chess

- Because skill at chess can be easily measured and subjected to laboratory experiments, the game has become an important test bed for theories in cognitive science.

- Researchers have found evidence that chess grandmasters rely on a vast store of knowledge of game positions. Some scientists have theorized that grandmasters organize the information in chunks, which can be quickly retrieved from long-term memory and manipulated in working memory.

- To accumulate this body of structured knowledge, grandmasters typically engage in years of effortful study, continually tackling challenges that lie just beyond their competence. The top performers in music, mathematics and sports appear to gain their expertise in the same way, motivated by competition and the joy of victory.

Garry Kasparov, the Russian grandmaster who has a rating of 2812, will win 75 percent of his games against the 100th-ranked grandmaster, Jan Timman of the Netherlands, who has a rating of 2616. Similarly, a U.S. tournament player rated 1200 (about the median) will win 75 percent of the time against someone rated 1000 (about the 40th percentile). Ratings allow psychologists to assess expertise by performance rather than reputation and to track changes in a given player's skill over the course of his or her career.

Another reason why cognitive scientists chose chess as their model—and not billiards, say, or bridge—is the game's reputation as, in German poet Johann Wolfgang von Goethe's words, "the touchstone of the intellect." The feats of chess masters have long been ascribed to nearly magical mental powers. This magic shines brightest in the so-called blindfold games in which the players are not allowed to see the board. In 1894 French psychologist Alfred Binet, the co-inventor of the first intelligence test, asked chess masters to describe how they played such games. He began with the hypothesis that they achieved an almost photographic image of the board, but he soon concluded that the visualization was much more abstract. Rather than seeing the knight's mane or the grain of the wood from which it is made, the master calls up only a general knowledge of where the piece stands in relation to other elements of the position. It is the same kind of implicit knowledge that the commuter has of the stops on a subway line.

The blindfolded master supplements such knowledge with details of the game at hand as well as with recollections of salient aspects of past games. Let us say he has somehow forgotten the precise position of a pawn. He can find it, as it were, by considering the stereotyped strategy of the opening—a well-studied phase of the game with a relatively limited number of options. Or he can remember the logic behind one of his earlier moves—say, by reasoning: "I could not capture his bishop two moves ago; therefore, that pawn must have been standing in the way. . . ." He does not have to remember every detail at all times, because he can reconstruct any particular detail whenever he wishes by tapping a well-organized system of connections.

Of course, if the possession of such intricately structured knowledge explains not only success at blindfold play but also other abilities of chess masters, such as calculation and planning, then expertise in the game would depend not so much on innate abilities as on specialized training. Dutch psychologist Adriaan de Groot, himself a chess master, confirmed this notion in 1938, when he took advantage of the staging of a great international tournament in Holland to compare average and strong players with the world's leading grandmasters. One way he did so was to ask the players to describe their thoughts as they examined a position taken from a tournament game. He found that although experts—the class just below master—did analyze considerably more possibilities than the very weak players, there was little further increase in analysis as playing strength rose to the master and grandmaster levels. The better players did not examine more possibilities, only better ones—just as Capablanca had claimed.

Recent research has shown that de Groot's findings reflected in part the nature of his chosen test positions. A position in which extensive, accurate calculation is critical will allow the grandmasters to show their stuff, as it were, and they will then search more deeply along the branching tree of possible moves than the amateur can hope to do. So, too, experienced physicists may on occasion examine more possibilities than physics students do. Yet in both cases, the expert relies not so much on an intrinsically stronger power of analysis as on a store of structured knowledge. When confronted with a difficult position, a weaker player may calculate for half an hour, often looking many moves ahead, yet miss the right continuation, whereas a grandmaster sees the move immediately, without consciously analyzing anything at all.

De Groot also had his subjects examine a position for a limited period and then try to reconstruct it from memory. Performance at this task tracked game-playing strength all the way from novice to grandmaster. Beginners could not recall more than a very few details of the position, even after having examined it for 30 seconds, whereas grandmasters could usually get it perfectly, even if they had perused it for only a few seconds. This difference tracks a particular form of memory, specific to the kind of chess positions that commonly occur in play. The specific memory must be the result of training, because grandmasters do no better than others in general tests of memory.

Similar results have been demonstrated in bridge players (who can remember cards played in many games), computer programmers (who can reconstruct masses of computer code) and musicians (who can recall long snatches of music). Indeed, such a memory for the subject matter of a particular field is a standard test for the existence of expertise.

The conclusion that experts rely more on structured knowledge than on analysis is supported by a rare case study of an initially weak chess player, identified only

A Grandmaster's Memory

Experiments indicate that the memory of chess masters is tuned to typical game positions. In 13 studies conducted between 1973 and 1996 (the results were compiled in a review article published in 1996), players at various skill levels were shown positions from actual games (*a*) and positions obtained by randomly shuffling the pieces (*b*). After observing the positions for 10 seconds or less, the players were asked to reconstruct them from memory. The results (*graph at bottom*) showed that chess masters (with ratings of 2200 or higher) and grandmasters (generally 2500 or higher) were significantly better than weaker players at recalling the game positions but only marginally better at remembering the random positions. This finely tuned long-term memory appears to be crucial to chess expertise.

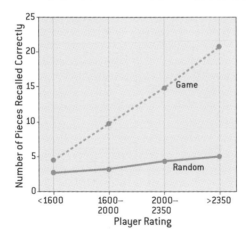

A structured knowledge of chess positions enables a grandmaster to spot the correct move quickly. The position above comes from a famous 1889 game between Emanuel Lasker (*white*) and Johann Bauer (*black*). Although a novice player would have to analyze the position extensively to see the winning move for white, any grandmaster would immediately recognize it. The correct move is shown in "White's Winning Move" box on page 100.

by the initials D.H., who over the course of nine years rose to become one of Canada's leading masters by 1987. Neil Charness, professor of psychology at Florida State University, showed that despite the increase in the player's strength, he analyzed chess positions no more extensively than he had earlier, relying instead on a vastly improved knowledge of chess positions and associated strategies.

Chunking Theory

In the 1960s Herbert A. Simon and William Chase, both at Carnegie Mellon University, tried to get a better understanding of expert memory by studying its limitations. Picking up where de Groot left off, they asked players of various strengths to reconstruct chess positions that had been artificially devised—that is, with the pieces placed randomly on the board—rather than reached as the result of master play [see "A Grandmaster's Memory" box]. The correlation between game-playing strength and the accuracy of the players' recall was much weaker with the random positions than with the authentic ones.

Chess memory was thus shown to be even more specific than it had seemed, being tuned not merely to the game itself but to typical chess positions. These experiments corroborated earlier studies that had demonstrated convincingly that ability in one area tends not to transfer to another. American psychologist Edward Thorndike first noted this lack of transference over a century ago, when he showed that the study of Latin, for instance, did not improve command of English and that geometric proofs do not teach the use of logic in daily life.

Simon explained the masters' relative weakness in reconstructing artificial chess positions with a model based on meaningful patterns called chunks. He invoked the concept to explain how chess masters can manipulate vast amounts of stored information, a task that would seem to strain the working memory. Psychologist George Miller of Princeton University famously estimated the limits of working memory—the scratch pad of the

mind—in a 1956 paper entitled "The Magical Number
Seven, Plus or Minus Two." Miller showed that people
can contemplate only five to nine items at a time. By
packing hierarchies of information into chunks, Simon
argued, chess masters could get around this limitation,
because by using this method, they could access five
to nine chunks rather than the same number of smaller
details.

Take the sentence "Mary had a little lamb."
The number of information chunks in this sentence
depends on one's knowledge of the poem and the
English language. For most native speakers of English,
the sentence is part of a much larger chunk, the familiar
poem. For someone who knows English but not the
poem, the sentence is a single, self-contained chunk.
For someone who has memorized the words but not
their meaning, the sentence is five chunks, and it is
18 chunks for someone who knows the letters but
not the words.

In the context of chess, the same differences can be
seen between novices and grandmasters. To a beginner,
a position with 20 chessmen on the board may contain
far more than 20 chunks of information, because the
pieces can be placed in so many configurations. A
grandmaster, however, may see one part of the position
as "fianchettoed bishop in the castled kingside,"
together with a "blockaded king's-Indian-style pawn
chain," and thereby cram the entire position into
perhaps five or six chunks. By measuring the time it

takes to commit a new chunk to memory and the number of hours a player must study chess before reaching grandmaster strength, Simon estimated that a typical grandmaster has access to roughly 50,000 to 100,000 chunks of chess information. A grandmaster can retrieve any of these chunks from memory simply by looking at a chess position, in the same way that most native English speakers can recite the poem "Mary had a little lamb" after hearing just the first few words.

Even so, there were difficulties with chunking theory. It could not fully explain some aspects of memory, such as the ability of experts to perform their feats while being distracted (a favorite tactic in the study of memory). K. Anders Ericsson of Florida State University and Charness argued that there must be some other mechanism that enables experts to employ long-term memory as if it, too, were a scratch pad. Says Ericsson: "The mere demonstration that highly skilled players can play at almost their normal strength under blindfold conditions is almost impossible for chunking theory to explain because you have to know the position, then you have to explore it in your memory." Such manipulation involves changing the stored chunks, at least in some ways, a task that may be likened to reciting "Mary had a little lamb" backward. It can be done, but not easily, and certainly not without many false starts and errors. Yet grandmaster games played quickly and under blindfold conditions tend to be of surprisingly high quality.

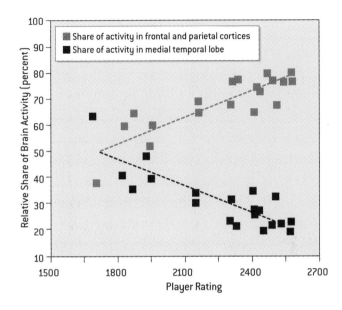

Brain activity in chess masters is different from the pattern observed in novices. In a 2001 report researchers used magnetoencephalography—the measurement of magnetic fields produced by electric currents in the brain—on subjects playing chess against a computer. In weaker players more activity occurred in the brain's medial temporal lobe than in the frontal and parietal cortices, which suggests that the amateurs were analyzing unusual new moves. In grandmasters, however, the frontal and parietal cortices were more active, indicating that they were retrieving information from long-term memory.

Ericsson also cites studies of physicians who clearly put information into long-term memory and take it out again in ways that enable them to make diagnoses. Perhaps Ericsson's most homely example, though, comes from reading. In a 1995 study he and Walter Kintsch of the University of Colorado found that interrupting highly proficient readers hardly slowed their reentry to a text; in the end, they lost only a few seconds. The researchers explained these findings by recourse to a structure they called long-term working memory, an almost oxymoronic coinage because it assigns to long-term memory the one thing that had always been defined as incompatible with it: thinking. But brain-imaging studies done in 2001 at the University of Konstanz in Germany provide support for the theory by showing that expert chess players activate long-term memory much more than novices do [see "Brain Activity" illustration].

Fernand Gobet of Brunel University in London champions a rival theory, devised with Simon in the late 1990s. It extends the idea of chunks by invoking highly characteristic and very large patterns consisting of perhaps a dozen chess pieces. Such a template, as they call it, would have a number of slots into which the master could plug such variables as a pawn or a bishop. A template might exist, say, for the concept of "the isolated queen's-pawn position from the Nimzo-Indian Defense," and a master might change a slot by reclassifying it as the same position "minus the dark-squared bishops." To resort again to the poetic analogy, it would be a bit like memorizing a riff on "Mary had a little lamb" by substituting rhyming equivalents at certain slots, such as "Larry" for "Mary," "pool" for "school" and so on. Anyone who knows the original template should be able to fix the altered one in memory in a trice.

A Proliferation of Prodigies

The one thing that all expertise theorists agree on is that it takes enormous effort to build these structures in the mind. Simon coined a psychological law of his own, the 10-year rule, which states that it takes approximately a decade of heavy labor to master any field. Even child prodigies, such as Gauss in mathematics, Mozart in music and Bobby Fischer in chess, must have made an equivalent effort, perhaps by starting earlier and working harder than others.

According to this view, the proliferation of chess prodigies in recent years merely reflects the advent of computer-based training methods that let children study far more master games and to play far more frequently against master-strength programs than their forerunners could typically manage. Fischer made a sensation when he achieved the grandmaster title at age 15, in 1958; today's record-holder, Sergey Karjakin of Ukraine, earned it at 12 years, seven months.

Ericsson argues that what matters is not experience per se but "effortful study," which entails continually tackling challenges that lie just beyond one's competence. That is why it is possible for enthusiasts to spend tens of thousands of hours playing chess or golf or a musical instrument without ever advancing beyond the amateur

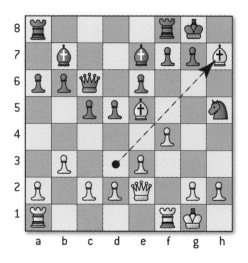

White's winning move is bishop takes pawn on the h7 square. Black's king then captures the bishop, and the white queen captures the black knight at h5, with check, forcing the black king back to g8. White's other bishop then captures the pawn on g7, where it is taken by the black king. The double-bishop sacrifice paves the way for a queen-and-rook attack, forcing black to give up his queen to stave off mate. Emanuel Lasker, the game's winner, went on to become the world chess champion in 1894, a title he retained for 27 years before losing to José Raúl Capablanca.

level and why a properly trained student can overtake them in a relatively short time. It is interesting to note that time spent playing chess, even in tournaments, appears to contribute less than such study to a player's progress; the main training value of such games is to point up weaknesses for future study.

Even the novice engages in effortful study at first, which is why beginners so often improve rapidly in playing golf, say, or in driving a car. But having reached an acceptable performance—for instance, keeping up with one's golf buddies or passing a driver's exam—most people relax. Their performance then becomes automatic and therefore impervious to further improvement. In contrast, experts-in-training keep the lid of their mind's box open all the time, so that they can inspect, criticize and augment its contents and thereby approach the standard set by leaders in their fields.

Meanwhile the standards denoting expertise grow ever more challenging. High school runners manage the four-minute mile; conservatory students play pieces once attempted only by virtuosi. Yet it is chess, again, that offers the most convincing comparison over time. John Nunn, a British mathematician who is also a grandmaster, recently used a computer to help him compare the errors committed in all the games in two international tournaments, one held in 1911, the other in 1993. The modern players played far more accurately. Nunn then examined all the games of one player in 1911 who scored in the middle of the pack and concluded that his rating today would be no better than 2100, hundreds of points below the grandmaster level—"and that was on a good day and with a following wind." The very best old-time masters were considerably stronger but still well below the level of today's leaders.

Then again, Capablanca and his contemporaries had neither computers nor game databases. They had to work things out for themselves, as did Bach, Mozart and Beethoven, and if they fall below today's masters in technique, they tower above them in creative power. The same comparison can be made between Newton and the typical newly minted Ph.D. in physics.

At this point, many skeptics will finally lose patience. Surely, they will say, it takes more to get to Carnegie Hall than practice, practice, practice. Yet this belief in the importance of innate talent, strongest perhaps among the experts themselves and their trainers, is strangely lacking in hard evidence to substantiate it. In 2002 Gobet conducted a study of British chess players ranging from amateurs to grandmasters and found no connection at all between their playing strengths and their visual-spatial abilities, as measured by shape-memory tests. Other researchers have found that the abilities of professional handicappers to predict the results of horse races did not correlate at all with their mathematical abilities.

Although nobody has yet been able to predict who will become a great expert in any field, a notable experiment has shown the possibility of deliberately creating one. László Polgár, an educator in Hungary, homeschooled his three daughters in chess, assigning as much as six hours of work a day, producing one inter-national master and two grandmasters—the strongest chess-playing siblings in history. The youngest Polgár, 30-year-old Judit, is now ranked 14th in the world.

The Polgár experiment proved two things: that grandmasters can be reared and that women can be grandmasters. It is no coincidence that the incidence

Training Trumps Talent

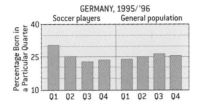

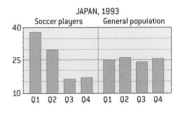

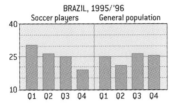

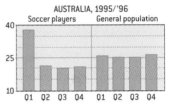

A 1999 study of professional soccer players suggests that they owe their success more to training than to talent. In Germany, Brazil, Japan and Australia, the players were much more likely than average to have been born in the first quarter (*Q1*) after the cutoff date for youth soccer leagues (*graphs above*). Because these players were older than their teammates when they joined the leagues, they would have enjoyed advantages in size and strength, allowing them to handle the ball and score more often. Their success in early years would have motivated them to keep improving, thus explaining their disproportionate representation in the professional leagues.

of chess prodigies multiplied after László Polgár published a book on chess education. The number of musical prodigies underwent a similar increase after Mozart's father did the equivalent two centuries earlier.

Thus, motivation appears to be a more important factor than innate ability in the development of expertise.

It is no accident that in music, chess and sports—all domains in which expertise is defined by competitive performance rather than academic credentialing— professionalism has been emerging at ever younger ages, under the ministrations of increasingly dedicated parents and even extended families.

Furthermore, success builds on success, because each accomplishment can strengthen a child's motivation. A 1999 study of professional soccer players from several countries showed that they were much more likely than the general population to have been born at a time of year that would have dictated their enrollment in youth soccer leagues at ages older than the average [see "Training Trumps Talent" box]. In their early years, these children would have enjoyed a substantial advantage in size and strength when playing soccer with their teammates. Because the larger, more agile children would get more opportunities to handle the ball, they would score more often, and their success at the game would motivate them to become even better.

Teachers in sports, music and other fields tend to believe that talent matters and that they know it when they see it. In fact, they appear to be confusing ability with precocity. There is usually no way to tell, from a recital alone, whether a young violinist's extraordinary performance stems from innate ability or from years of Suzuki-style training. Capablanca, regarded to this day as the greatest "natural" chess player, boasted that he never studied the game. In fact, he flunked out of

Columbia University in part because he spent so much time playing chess. His famously quick apprehension was a product of all his training, not a substitute for it.

The preponderance of psychological evidence indicates that experts are made, not born. What is more, the demonstrated ability to turn a child quickly into an expert—in chess, music and a host of other subjects—sets a clear challenge before the schools. Can educators find ways to encourage students to engage in the kind of effortful study that will improve their reading and math skills? Roland G. Fryer, Jr., an economist at Harvard University, has experimented with offering monetary rewards to motivate students in underperforming schools in New York City and Dallas. In one ongoing program in New York, for example, teachers test the students every three weeks and award small amounts—on the order of $10 or $20—to those who score well. The early results have been promising. Instead of perpetually pondering the question, "Why can't Johnny read?" perhaps educators should ask, "Why should there be anything in the world he can't learn to do?"

More to Explore

The Rating of Chessplayers, Past and Present. Arpad E. Elo. Arco Publishing, 1978.

Thought and Choice in Chess. Adriaan de Groot. Mouton de Gruyter, 1978.

Expert Performance in Sports: Advances in Research on Sport Expertise. Edited by Janet L. Starkes and K. Anders Ericsson. Human Kinetics, 2003.

Moves in Mind: The Psychology of Board Games. Fernand Gobet, Alex de Voogt and Jean Retschitzki. Psychology Press, 2004.

The Cambridge Handbook of Expertise and Expert Performance. Edited by K. Anders Ericsson, Paul J. Feltovich, Robert R. Hoffman and Neil Charness. Cambridge University Press, 2006.

About the Author

PHILIP E. ROSS, a contributing editor at *Scientific American*, is a chess player himself and father of Laura Ross, a master who outranks him by 199 points.

WEB SITES

Due to the changing nature of Internet links, Rosen Publishing has developed an online list of Web sites related to the subject of this book. This site is updated regularly. Please use this link to access the list:

http://www.rosenlinks.com/saces/wmge

For Further Reading

Andreasen, Nancy A. *The Creating Brain: The Neuroscience of Genius.* New York, NY: Dana Press, 2005.

Andreasen, Nancy A. *The Creative Brain: The Science of Genius.* New York, NY: Plume, 2006.

Jamison, Kay Redfield. *Touched with Fire: Manic-Depressive Illness and the Artistic Temperament.* New York, NY: Free Press, 1996.

Peek, Fran. *The Real Rain Man: Kim Peek.* Salt Lake City, UT: Harkness, 1997.

Schenk, David. *The Immortal Game: A History of Chess, or How 32 Carved Pieces on a Board Illuminated Our Understanding of War, Art, Science and the Human Brain.* New York, NY: Doubleday, 2006.

Sforza, Teri, Howard Lenhoff, and Sylvia Lenhoff. *The (Strangest) Song: One Father's Quest to Help His Daughter Find Her Voice.* Amherst, NY: Prometheus Books, 2006.

Tammett, Daniel. *Born on a Blue Day: Inside the Extraordinary Mind of an Autistic Savant.* New York, NY: Free Press, 2007.

Treffert, Darold. A. *Extraordinary People: Understanding Savant Syndrome.* iUniverse.com, Inc., 2000.

Winner, Ellen. *Gifted Children: Myths and Realities.* New York, NY: Basic Books, 1997.

INDEX